A PRACTICAL GUIDE TO

Collateral Management in the OTC Derivatives Market

Edited by

PENNY DAVENPORT

First published 2003 by
PALGRAVE MACMILLAN
Houndmills, Basingstoke, Hampshire RG21 6XS and
175 Fifth Avenue, New York, N.Y. 10010
Companies and representatives throughout the world

PALGRAVE MACMILLAN is the global academic imprint of the Palgrave
Macmillan division of St. Martin's Press, LLC and of Palgrave Macmillan Ltd.
Macmillan® is a registered trademark in the United States, United Kingdom
and other countries. Palgrave is a registered trademark in the European
Union and other countries.

ISBN 1–4039–1203–3

This book is printed on paper suitable for recycling and made from fully
managed and sustained forest sources.

A catalogue record for this book is available from the British Library.

Library of Congress Cataloging-in-Publication Data

A practical guide to collateral management in the OTC derivatives market /
edited by Penny Davenport.
    p. cm. — (Finance and capital markets)
Includes bibliographical references and index.
  ISBN 1–4039–1203–3
  1. Derivative securities. 2. Over-the-counter markets. 3. Credit—
Management. I. Davenport, Penny. II. Series.
  HG6024.3 .P7 2003
  332. 64'5—dc21

                                                            2003050450

Editing and origination by Aardvark Editorial, Mendham, Suffolk

10 9 8 7 6 5 4 3 2 1
12 11 10 09 08 07 06 05 04 03

Transferred to digital printing in 2007.

CONTENTS

LIST OF FIGURES

LIST OF TABLES

PREFACE

The use of collateral management in the OTC Derivatives markets as a credit risk mitigation and a business development technique has increased dramatically over the past ten years. The International Swaps and Derivatives Association (ISDA) estimated that the total amount of collateral in the derivatives markets in 2002 exceeded $437 billion, representing a 75% increase on 2001.[1] The increase between 2000 and 2001 was 25%. As collateral management in the OTC Derivatives markets has grown in popularity, so more firms have become engaged in the process. Collateral management, for any product set, is a multifunctional discipline and for each firm involved in the giving and receiving of collateral, you can multiply that number by several times to determine the number of individuals on whom collateral management has an impact on any given day. This book is written for those people.

A Practical Guide to Collateral Management in the OTC Derivatives Market is written for anyone who comes into contact with the collateral management process during their daily working lives. This might include collateral professionals who spend their time in a centralised collateral management function or support unit. It might also include a senior operations manager who has the responsibility for the collateral management function as part of his or her remit.

Other people impacted by the collateral management process include:

- Lawyers, and derivatives and collateral documentation specialists
- Credit risk managers and loan officers
- Portfolio managers
- Custodial specialists
- Middle-office personnel

▓ Accounting and tax functions

▓ Traders, marketers and sales desks.

The process of collateral management is often intellectualised by some who enjoy pushing the boundaries of their own thinking. There are also those who thrive on making collateral management processes appear significantly more complicated than they are in reality, typically to shore up their own positions in their organisations or to extend their organisational empires. However, once the collateral management process has been broken down to the raw nuts and bolts, the fundamental principles and steps are actually quite simple.

This book uncovers the basic principles involved in the collateral management process and distils them down to the most basic levels.

This is helpful to promote a wider level of understanding. It will also give those who are building collateral management frameworks within firms the necessary building blocks to fulfil their responsibilities with confidence.

Of course, once people feel they have put those building blocks in place and have a good fundamental understanding of collateral management, or have built a foundation collateral management programme, they may wish to take things to a more sophisticated level. However, even then, the authors of this book would caution against being too clever or putting too complicated a framework around the collateral management process for the following reasons.

Collateral management is a risk transformation tool. The process of collateral management takes credit risk and exchanges it for other types of risk including legal risk and operational risk. These risks will be addressed in more detail during the course of this book but it is worth mentioning here that the more complicated the processes around collateral management, the higher the level of operational risk that can be introduced. Such increased levels of risk can undermine the value of having a collateral management programme in the first place.

Further, the more advanced the collateral management framework a firm has in place, the more resources, particularly people and technology, a firm is likely to be asked to invest. Firms are invariably cost conscious and need to undertake a rigorous cost-benefit analysis to determine if the increased expenditure that accompanies a more complicated business actually reaps dividends.

This book, therefore, keeps things simple and encourages those reading it to do the same. It is divided into three parts. Part I looks at some of the foundation concepts in collateral management; Part II looks in detail at setting up a collateral management programme and Part III reviews the after-effects of taking collateral.

ACKNOWLEDGEMENTS

This book has been a collaborative effort on the part of Lombard Risk Management from start to finish. However, we would like to recognise the leadership of John Wisbey, Chairman and CEO, in deciding that Lombard Risk would write this book and for his contribution to determining the content. John's executive team contributed wisdom and support. Specifically, generous recognition for their time and efforts is due to Charlotte Eaton, Mark Higgins, Diana Hutchison and Dr Lee Wakeman who each authored individual chapters of the book but worked in a true team effort to ensure a cohesive whole. Glennis Appannah, David Sadler and Andrea Hartill have been instrumental in preparing the final manuscript.

Finally, Lombard Risk is delighted to have had the opportunity of working with Clifford Chance in the development of this book. Habib Motani and Lynn Shouls specifically are the authors of Chapter 5 and we are pleased to have worked so closely with them and thank them for their time and expertise.

PENNY DAVENPORT
Author and Editor

LIST OF ACRONYMS

BBC	Bond borrow against cash
BBL	Bond Borrow/Loan
BLC	Bond loan against cash
BIS	Bank for International Settlements
BS	Buy Sell Backs
CLS	Continuous Linked Settlement
CSA	ISDA Credit Support Annex
DBV	Delivery by Value
DVP	Delivery versus Payment
ESLA	Equity Stock Lending Agreement
ETR	Elective Termination Rights
EUIR	The EU Insolvency Regulation
FB	Fee Borrow
FL	Fee Loan
FOP	Free of Payment
FSA	Financial Services Authority
FTSE 100	Financial Times Stock Exchange 100 Index
FX	Foreign Exchange
GESLA	Gilt Edged Stock Lending Agreement
GMRA	Global Master Repurchase Agreement
GMSLA	Global Master Stock Lending Agreement

IDNA	International Deposit Netting Agreement
IRB	International Ratings Based Approach
ISDA	International Swaps and Derivatives Association
ISLA	International Securities Lenders' Association
ISMA	International Securities Market Association
LOC	Letter of Credit
OSLA	Overseas Securities Lending Agreement
OTC Derivatives	Over the Counter Derivatives
PRIMA	Place of the Relevant Intermediary Approach
PSA	Public Securities Association
PVP	Payment versus Payment
R	Classic repo
Repo	Repurchase Agreement
RR	Reverse repo
RVP	Receipt versus Payment
SB	Sell Buy Backs
SB	Security Borrow
SBL	Stock Borrow/Loan
SL	Stock Loan
VAR	Value-at-Risk
WD(C)	Winding up Directive for Credit Institutions
WD(I)	Winding up Directive for Insurance Undertakings

PART I

Foundation Concepts in Collateral Management

INTRODUCTION

Chapter 1 introduces some of the key concepts in collateral management and sets the scene for the rest of the book.

WHAT IS COLLATERAL MANAGEMENT?

Collateral management is the practice of taking an asset, typically cash, securities, equities or property, as protection against a credit event such as an event of default. An everyday example might be the use of a house as security against a home loan or mortgage. Should the borrower fail to make mortgage repayments on time, the lender may seize the house and sell or liquidate it, and use the proceeds to offset the outstanding loan.

COLLATERAL MANAGEMENT IN THE OTC DERIVATIVES MARKETS

The practice of taking collateral in the OTC Derivatives markets has been widespread since the early nineties. In the OTC Derivatives markets, the exposure, which is the equivalent of the loan in the mortgage example (Figure 1.1), is created from a portfolio of derivatives transactions. The asset which is taken as collateral against that exposure is typically cash, securities such as government or corporate bonds, or equities. The key difference between taking a house as collateral against a home loan and taking collateral to offset the exposure generated by a portfolio of OTC Derivatives is the volatility of the underlying exposure. The amount of the exposure varies daily, or even intra-daily, and therefore the amount of collateral which is required also changes daily or intra-daily. This

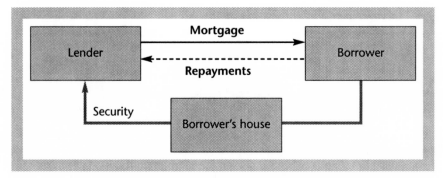

Figure 1.1 A traditional mortgage as an
example of a collateralised exposure

means that the process of managing collateral requirements for the OTC Derivatives markets is much more dynamic, and accordingly, more complex.

THE GROWTH OF COLLATERAL MANAGEMENT IN THE OTC DERIVATIVES MARKETS

In 2002 there was an estimated $437 billion of collateral in circulation in the OTC Derivatives markets.[2] This was up 75% on 2001 and 25% on 2000. The number of collateral agreements in use in 2001 was calculated to be more than 16,000 which was an increase of 45% on the year before; 21% of all collateral management programmes in 2001 supported more than 500 collateral agreements each.

This level of growth has been sustained year-on-year for the past decade and collateralisation has become the most popular technique for credit risk mitigation in the OTC Derivatives markets. The next section looks at some of the reasons for this growth.

KEY DRIVERS BEHIND THE GROWTH IN COLLATERAL MANAGEMENT

There have been a number of key reasons behind the growth in collateral management in the OTC Derivatives markets over the last decade (Table 1.1). These are summarised in this chapter and then addressed in more detail throughout the book.

1. Credit risk management
The primary reason behind the growth in collateral management has been a requirement to manage credit risk more actively. The respondents to the ISDA

Table 1.1 Relative rankings of key drivers for collateralisation

	2000 Ranking		2001 Ranking	Trend
Credit risk reductions	1	⟶	1	•⟶•
Regulatory capital savings	3	⟶	2	•⟋•
Increased competitiveness	4	⟶	3	•⟋•
Improved market liquidity	2	⟶	4	•⟍•
Access to more exotic business	5	⟶	5	•⟶•

Source: ISDA Margin 2000 Survey and 2001 Survey

Margin Survey 2001 cited this as the most important driver behind collateral management. Taking collateral will protect a firm against credit losses upon default.

2. Regulatory capital savings

Holdings of collateral can be used to offset regulatory capital requirements. Banking supervisors, globally, have invested a lot of time and research into the practices of collateral management in the OTC Derivatives markets and accordingly have become more willing to recognise the benefits of having collateral when calculating regulatory capital requirements. This topic is covered in more detail in Chapter 11.

3. Business expansion

The other key drivers covered in the ISDA survey can be wrapped up together under the heading of 'business expansion'. When collateral is taken under a collateral arrangement, firms can be more confident that they have something to rely on in the event of a counterparty's default and will use this confidence as a factor in the decision to undertake more business and a wider range of business including longer-dated, more exotic and risky structures.

4. Counterparty policy

Another reason behind the growth in collateral management is the requirement of certain types of counterparties including government agencies and supranational bodies who request the provision of collateral by specific counterparties, possibly on the grounds of their credit rating, or in support of certain types of transactions, for example longer-dated transactions.

Having reviewed the growth in the use of collateralisation in the OTC Derivatives markets, and some of the reasons behind the growth, Chapter 2 will review both the theory behind the practices and the actual practicalities of the collateralisation process.

THE THEORY AND PRACTICALITIES OF CREDIT RISK MITIGATION TECHNIQUES IN THE OTC DERIVATIVES MARKETS

Chapter 2 provides an introduction to the practice of portfolio collateralisation in the OTC Derivatives markets. Portfolio collateralisation is the most popular credit risk mitigation technique employed within the OTC Derivatives markets today. Chapter 2 is ideal for providing a thorough briefing for those who would like to know more about collateral or who have limited practical experience of the collateral management process.

Portfolio collateralisation limits the credit exposure of one or both parties, as defined within the credit support documentation, across an entire derivatives portfolio. The net market value of the portfolio is calculated, and if required, the out-of-the-money party must transfer collateral assets to the in-the-money party on the agreed portfolio review dates.[3] An in-depth review of portfolio collateralisation as a risk mitigation technique follows in the next section, which provides an interesting snapshot of the end-to-end process. While the concept of taking and giving collateral is a well-known and simple concept, the actual practices in the OTC Derivatives market can be somewhat removed from the theory. This will highlight those practices and provides some insight into the world of collateral from a practitioner's perspective.

OVERVIEW OF THE COLLATERAL MANAGEMENT PROCESS

Before reviewing each of the stages in the collateral management process in turn, we look first at those stages and the players in an organisation who might be involved at each stage (Table 2.1).

We now go on to review each of the steps in the process in turn, both from a theoretical perspective and in practice.

Make the decision to enter into a collateralised relationship

Today, as collateralisation in the OTC Derivatives markets is a widespread practice, more often than not the execution of a collateral agreement takes place at the outset of the relationship, when transacting with a new client for the first time. Collateralisation may even be mandatory under some corporate policies. However, in the past, when the practice of collateralisation was still on the increase, financial institutions typically have reviewed long-standing, previously uncollateralised relationships with a view to implementing credit support arrangements. This has often been done in large numbers, to meet the requirements laid out by credit risk managers to manage credit risk, or possibly traders wishing to expand the volumes, ranges and types of business.

Table 2.1 Stages in the collateral management process

Stage in the collateral management process	Players involved
Make the decision to enter into a collateralised relationship	Credit risk officer, business sponsor
Negotiate the terms of the collateral agreement	Lawyer, collateral manager, credit risk officer, business sponsor
Establish the new agreement in the collateral management system	Collateral manager
Make collateral calls and agree delivery and return amounts	Collateral manager
Settle collateral receipts and deliveries	Settlements
Update records to show changes in collateral balances	Collateral manager
Reflect collateral holdings in credit risk management systems	Collateral manager, credit risk officer
Collateral risk management	Collateral manager
Management reporting	Collateral manager

Example

In this example, Bank A would like to execute a long-dated transaction with a very large notional with Bank B. The two institutions have a long-standing business relationship which has traditionally consisted of low volume, short-dated business, for example, with maturities of less than 5 years, and carrying relatively low risk. The portfolio has been made up of a handful of interest rate and cross-currency swaps, with occasional FX transactions included for hedging purposes.

A trader at Bank A would like to trade a 20-year interest rate swap with Bank B. Although the two institutions have an excellent long-term relationship, the credit risk manager at Bank A who is responsible for Bank B is reluctant to trade a 20-year swap with Bank B on an unsecured basis. Why? Well, her thought process is that although Bank B is of good credit quality today, credit downgrades can happen quickly, and she does not have a crystal ball to help predict the financial health of Bank B in 10, 20 or 30 years' time. Therefore, the trader and the credit risk manager agree that Bank A can enter into a long-dated transaction with Bank B, under the condition that a collateral agreement is signed using industry standard credit support documentation such as the ISDA Credit Support Annex,[4] which is an annex to the ISDA Master. This situation is typical among many long-standing derivatives counterparties.

Although portfolio collateralisation using the ISDA Credit Support Annex is the most widely used credit risk mitigation technique in the OTC Derivatives market, there are other credit risk mitigation techniques that can be used under the right circumstances. These alternative methods are explored in Chapter 3, and their advantages and disadvantages are discussed briefly. In this chapter, we focus on the practices associated with portfolio collateralisation.

Negotiate the terms of the collateral agreement

In the case of an existing client relationship, once the decision has been made to collateralise a portfolio, usually by a credit risk manager in conjunction with a trader or business sponsor, steps must be taken to work with a client to agree to sign the collateral agreement. There are many factors which can persuade clients that signing a collateral agreement will be fruitful, including the fact that it will ultimately facilitate more, and more profitable business. This will be achieved through reductions in the cost of credit, freeing up trading lines and enabling both the bank and the client, typically, to make savings in regulatory capital. Many discussions with existing clients regarding signing collateral agreements are in the form of presentations to senior business sponsors, relationship managers and credit personnel by the collateral manager which emphasise some, or all, of the key benefits involved in signing a collateral agreement. While there are still some counterparties and clients today who will reject the actual concept of portfolio collateralisation for their OTC Derivatives transactions, the most common objections relate to the resource implications of establishing a collateral management infrastructure or the cost of sourcing collateral requirements.

In the instance that a client may be trading with an institution for the first time, the process of signing the collateral agreement is more 'organic' as collateralisation is the norm in the OTC Derivatives markets today. Therefore, the bank or party seeking collateralisation will spend less time and effort promoting the idea to the client of collateralising all future transactions.

Returning to our example where Bank A and Bank B have had a long-term trading relationship, the business sponsors at Bank A would not want to jeopardise any possible future business with Bank B, and will therefore tread carefully when initiating discussions about collateralising future long-dated transactions. Naturally, Bank B may be initially reluctant to enter into such an agreement, but the business sponsor and the credit officers will discuss the benefits that could be enjoyed as a result of signing a collateral agreement. Bank B will hopefully conclude that benefits could be realised in the form of increased trading lines, more competitive pricing and the promise that Bank A would grant them the right to re-use their collateral assets under the terms of the Credit Support Annex, enabling the value of any collateral which is pledged to them. Meanwhile, Bank A is able to execute lucrative long-term business on a risk-reduced basis.

The ISDA Master Agreement

In terms of documentation, the ISDA Master Agreement is an umbrella agreement that governs derivatives transactions between two parties, and is used widely by industry participants. ISDA has established international contractual standards governing privately negotiated derivatives transactions that reduce legal uncertainty and allow for reduction of credit risk through the netting of contractural obligations. This contract provides all users of derivatives (banks, broker-dealers, end-users and other financial institutions) an excellent framework from within which they can conduct business. This topic is discussed in greater detail in Chapter 5.

Figure 2.1 The ISDA Master Agreement

Assuming that a financial institution is already trading under an ISDA Master Agreement with a given counterparty (Figure 2.1), if it is deemed desirable to collateralise existing and future transactions on a portfolio basis, additional terms must be negotiated and drawn up in the form of a collateral agreement which most commonly takes the form of an ISDA Credit Support Annex (CSA). This annex serves as an addendum to the original Master agreement and details, in full, the basis on which the portfolio will be collateralised. Ordinarily, at this stage, credit risk managers, lawyers, business sponsors and the collateral manager will work together to negotiate the parameters of the agreement with the client. Any institution actively seeking to participate in derivatives transactions should consider defining a firm-wide collateral policy prior to engaging in business to minimise the potentially long, and time-consuming process, of negotiating the agreement with the counterparty or client. The policy should detail the industry best practices as a benchmark, the best practice or realistic standard for the individual firm concerned, and the individuals or groups of people (for example credit risk managers) who may approve deviations from the policy. This topic is addressed in more detail in Chapter 7.

Establish the new agreement in the collateral management system

Once the agreement has been fully executed, which means that terms have been agreed, and the paperwork has been signed and returned by a client, it is now legally binding and collateralisation of transactions can begin immediately. At this stage, the collateral practitioner is required to extract the key terms from the collateral agreement and to transfer them, either manually or in an automated way, to the collateral management system or spreadsheet. An absence of adequate technology to support collateral agreements is a common cause of disruption to an otherwise smooth start, but further, a lack of practical knowledge can also cause problems. This creates additional work for institutions as they try to define their collateral policy and implement a collateral management programme while simultaneously struggling to cope with the demands of new technology, processes and documentation.

In order to calculate an accurate margin call, several factors have to be considered:

- A counterparty's exposure, which is the net mark-to-market[5] value of all OTC Derivatives transactions between the two parties, under the ISDA CSA

- The value of any collateral held or delivered

- The terms of the CSA.

The calculations can become relatively complex, but for a small number of agreements, they can still be performed on a spreadsheet. However, more robust technology offers enormous convenience in terms of storing agreement terms, archiving margin call statements, reporting capabilities and general audit facilities, and it is these factors which attract an institution into investing in a specialised collateral management application. This is addressed in more detail in Chapter 8.

Many firms transfer the terms of the CSA into the collateral management system manually. This is sustainable for a small number of agreements but is not effective for a large number of agreements. As firms grow and become more sophisticated they can automate the process of transposing terms from a documentation repository, either in-house or a commercial solution, into the collateral management system.

Whichever process an individual firm follows, the important thing is that there is an independent review of the terms of the CSA in the collateral management system. This is a key control to minimise operating errors in the collateral management process. For example, if a credit risk manager has agreed an unsecured threshold of £1,000,000, care must be taken to ensure this is not input as £10,000,000.

Make collateral calls and agree delivery and return amounts

In order to calculate a margin requirement, it must first be determined whether the total mark-to-market exposure for any given collateral arrangement is in-the-money or out-of-the-money from the perspective of the calculation agent, who will be referred to here as the principal party.

In the event that the mark-to-market exposure is positive or in-the-money to the principal party, the following calculation must be applied to determine whether a collateral deficit or excess exists for that particular agreement:

Positive Mark-to-Market Exposure + P.I.A − C.I.A = Total Exposure Amount

If Total Exposure Amount >C.Thr (Total Exposure Amount − C.Thr = Adj.Exp.Amt, 0)

Adj.Exp.Amt − Coll.H + Coll.D = Net.Margin.Req

If Net.Margin.Req > C.MTA (Net.Margin.Req, 0)

If Net.Margin.Req >0 (Collateral owed P, Collateral owed C)

And under the terms of the ISDA 2001 Margin Provisions only:

If Net.Margin.Req >0 (Collateral owed P = Net.Margin.Req + P.L.M.Req and Collateral owed C = C.L.M.Req, Collateral owed P = P.L.M.Req and Collateral owed C = Net.Margin.Req + C.L.M.Req)

Where:

P.I.A = Principal Independent Amount

C.I.A = Counterparty Independent Amount

C.Thr = Counterparty Threshold

P.Thr = Principal Threshold

Adj.Exp.Amt = Adjusted Exposure Amount

Net.Margin.Req = Net Margin Requirement

Coll.H = Collateral Held

Coll.D = Collateral Delivered

C.MTA = Counterparty Minimum Transfer Amount

P.MTA = Principal Minimum Transfer Amount

P = Principal

C= Counterparty

If however, the mark-to-market exposure is negative or out-of-the-money, the calculations performed would be the inverse of those previously defined:

Negative Mark-to-Market Exposure – P.I.A + C.I.A = Total.Exp.Amt

If Total.Exp.Amt< P.Thr (Total.Exp.Amt+P.Thr = Adj.Exp.Amt, 0)

Adj.Exp.Amt + Coll.H – Coll.D = Net.Margin.Req

If Net.Margin.Req> P.MTA (Net.Margin.Req, 0)

If Net.Margin.Req <0 (Collateral owed C, Collateral owed P)

And under the terms of the ISDA 2001 Margin Provisions only:

If Net.Margin.Req <0 (Collateral owed C = Net.Margin.Req + C.L.M.Req and Collateral owed P = P.L.M.Req, Collateral owed C = C.L.M.Req and Collateral owed P = Net.Margin.Req + P.L.M.Req)

It should be noted that under the ISDA 2001 Margin Provisions, Lock Up Margin is not added to or subtracted from Independent Amounts or mark-to-market exposure. These terms will be addressed in more detail in Chapter 5 when we review the key forms of documentation which are used to document collateral management arrangements.

Collateral movement scenarios

There are five scenarios that can occur as a result of the margin calculation process:

1. The principal makes a demand for collateral from the counterparty

2. The principal makes a demand for a return of collateral currently delivered to the counterparty

3. The counterparty makes a demand for collateral from the principal

4. The counterparty makes a demand for a return of collateral currently delivered to the principal

5. No movement of collateral is required on either side.

Two scenarios may occur at the same time: that is, Scenario 2 where the principal makes a demand for the return of collateral currently pledged to the counterparty could be combined with Scenario 1 where the principal makes a demand for new collateral from the counterparty.

A clear distinction must be made between the five scenarios when issuing a collateral demand statement. Collateral technology employed to manage these calculations needs to clearly define ownership of the collateral, and therefore the type of movement required when a statement is generated and a demand ensues. For example, a collateral demand statement should clearly state which party is due to return or deliver collateral assets. The following section takes a closer look at the scenarios outlined above, and adds some practical perspective of some typical business experiences associated with these types of collateral movements.

Scenario 1: *The principal makes a demand for collateral from the counterparty*

In this example, the principal party's portfolio is in-the-money when calculated on a net basis, and the counterparty's threshold has been breached. The minimum call amount has been exceeded, and a rounding amount must also be applied to the margin call amount.[6] As a result of these calculations, a delivery of new assets must be made by the counterparty to the principal. The following calculations provide a breakdown of how a portfolio valuation generates such a requirement.

Example a: *Out-of-the-money exposure moves through zero to in-the-money exposure*

In the following example, we assume that the last portfolio valuation produced a net exposure that was in-the-money to the counterparty. As a result, the principal was required to deliver collateral to the counterparty to secure the exposure. The most recent valuation (presented below) clearly highlights the fact that there has been a large swing in the net exposure which is now in-the-money to the principal. So, this time, the counterparty must fulfil a collateral obligation, and additionally return any assets that were pledged by the principal last time to cover the previous requirement.
In short:

Exposure $14,857,943
Threshold ($10,000,000)
Assets (Held)/Delivered $3,000,000
Minimum Call Amount $100,000
Rounding Amount $10,000

Margin Call Amount: $3,000,000 to be returned to the principal, $4,860,000 to be delivered to the principal

Example b: *In-the-money exposure breaches threshold and requires delivery of collateral*

Example b illustrates how the portfolio exposure breaches the counterparty threshold for the first time, and a collateral requirement results:

Exposure $11,152,134
Threshold ($10,000,000)
Assets (Held)/Pledged $0
Minimum Call Amount $100,000
Rounding Amount $10,000

Margin Call Amount: $1,150,000 to be delivered to the principal

Scenario 2: *The principal makes a demand for a return of collateral currently delivered to the counterparty*

The principal party's portfolio is out-of-the-money, and their unsecured threshold has been breached. As a result, collateral in the amount of $2,000,000 has been delivered to the counterparty. The market value of the portfolio has decreased, and the minimum call amount has been exceeded, and so collateral must be returned to the principal. The rounding amount must be applied to the final call amount.

Example c: *Out-of-the-money exposure decreases and requires a return of collateral to the principal*

Exposure ($8,035,246)
Threshold $6,000,000
Assets (Held)/Pledged $3,000,000
Minimum Call Amount $100,000
Rounding Amount $10,000

Margin Call Amount: $960,000 to be returned to the principal

Scenario 3: *The counterparty makes a demand for collateral from the principal*

In this instance, the principal party's portfolio is out-of-the-money when calculated on a net basis, and the counterparty threshold has been breached. The minimum call amount has been exceeded, and a rounding amount must also be applied to the margin call amount. As a result of these calculations, a delivery of new collateral assets must be made to the principal by the counterparty. The following calculations provide a breakdown of how a portfolio valuation generates such a requirement:

Example d: *Out-of-the-money exposure requires an additional delivery of collateral*

In example d, the calculations illustrate how an increase in portfolio exposure requires a delivery of additional collateral by the principal:

Exposure ($17,628,462)
Threshold $12,000,000
Assets (Held)/Pledged $3,600,000
Minimum Call Amount $500,000
Rounding Amount $10,000

Margin Call Amount: $2,030,000 to be delivered to counterparty

Scenario 4: *The counterparty makes a demand for a return of collateral currently delivered to the principal*

The principal party's portfolio is in-the-money, and the counterparty threshold has been breached. As a result, collateral in the amount of $5,000,000 has been delivered to the principal. The market value of the portfolio has decreased and has fallen below the threshold, and so all the collateral which is being held must be returned to the counterparty.

Example e: *In-the-money exposure decreases significantly enough for exposure to be covered by the threshold, and requires a return of all the collateral*

Exposure $19,482,435
Threshold ($20,000,000)
Assets (Held)/Pledged ($930,000)
Minimum Call Amount $500,000
Rounding Amount $10,000

Margin Call Amount: $930,000 to be returned to the counterparty

Scenario 5: *No movement of collateral is required on either side*

There are two examples that may be associated with this scenario. The first is where a party's threshold has not yet been breached given the exposure that exists and so no movement of collateral is required. The second is where a party's threshold may have been breached, but the amount of exposure that breaches the threshold does not meet the minimum call amount, and so, no movement of collateral is required.

Example f: *No movement of collateral is required because threshold has not been breached*

Exposure $14,995,864
Threshold $15,000,000
Assets (Held)/Pledged $0
Minimum Call Amount $500,000
Rounding Amount $10,000

Margin Call Amount: $0 to be delivered to principal

Example g: *No movement of collateral is required because minimum call amount has not been breached*

Exposure $15,483,452
Threshold $15,000,000
Assets (Held)/Pledged $0
Minimum Call Amount $500,000
Rounding Amount $10,000

Margin Call Amount: $0 to be delivered to principal

Make collateral calls and agree collateral movements

In the event that a movement of collateral is required, the demand amount must be communicated to, and approved by, the recipient of the margin call. This is typically done by fax, e-mail or via a secure web page and is almost always followed up with a telephone call. It is important that the asset type to be delivered or returned (that is, bonds or cash) has been specified in the CSA and both parties agree the notional amount. The market value of the assets with any valuation percentages applied (collateral haircuts) must adequately cover the final call amount. Once the details of the movement have been agreed, both parties must instruct their custodians in order to action the delivery or receipt of assets out of, or into, the relevant account.

On a general note, if collateral assets are taken under a pledge agreement, they should be, in principle, held in safekeeping in segregated custody accounts. If assets are taken under a title transfer agreement, they should be pooled with the rest of the firm's assets, as the ownership of the collateral assets effectively transfers from the giver to the taker. Collateral which is taken under a pledge agreement may be available for re-use (also known as rehypothecation) under the terms of the CSA, in which case it will also be frequently commingled with the party's own assets. Therefore, collateral assets which are pledged and can be rehypothecated, and assets taken under a title transfer agreement, need to be tracked carefully and separately to ensure they are ultimately attributed back to the delivering party.

The decision makers behind the choice of collateral assets used to fund a collateral requirement vary from one institution to another. Commonly, a firm's repo desk will have considerable input or responsibility when delivering or sourcing securities. This can be more efficient than having that control within the collateral management unit as a repo trader is much more likely to have a good handle on which assets are the cheapest to deliver and so be able to achieve an optimisation of collateral assets. However, this means that the collateral management team do not have much control over the selection of which assets they send out.

In terms of physically instructing for the movement of securities, this again depends upon individual circumstances. Some institutions require that the repo desk maintains absolute control over their collateral assets, and manage the entire process down to instructing for movements of collateral out to counterparties. Other firms only involve the repo desks and only get involved when an institution requires additional assets to be sourced over and above what the collateral management function has control over. Common practice also differs among institutions as to whether collateral assets may require an internal transfer to a 'collateral book' before distribution to those counterparties which have a collateral requirement. Sourcing collateral assets and managing collateral which has been delivered is addressed in detail in Chapter 9.

Settle collateral receipts and deliveries

Once a margin requirement has been communicated to, and agreed by, a client, instructions must be forwarded to a firm's custody area to either receive or deliver the assets into an account. These instructions can be communicated either verbally, by fax, or e-mail but increasingly, collateral systems are built with custodial interfaces that allow for direct transmission of margin movement information. Such custodial interfaces streamline the margin call settlement process, allowing users to register any new assets which are delivered, automatically generate custodial advice notices, and deliver communications to the custody area instructing them of the movements.

The information flow can also be reversed, and custody systems relay information back to the collateral system, providing real-time updates of collateral positions, asset valuations, collateral in transit and also notifying users of failed margin movements. This reverse flow of information is critical in communicating to an institution whether a counterparty has settled their collateral movements on time and this information needs immediate escalation to a senior collateral manager or credit risk officer in the event of a failure. Although, on occasion, collateral settlements do fail for operational reasons, frequently a failure to deliver a collateral amount can be an early warning of liquidity pressure or other financial health strains at the counterparty and should be taken very seriously.

In the event that a custodial interface is not possible due to technology constraints, most collateral systems will allow users to manually update, or upload via spreadsheets, collateral data in order to record counterparty collateral holdings and the subsequent impact those holdings have on credit risk and exposure.

Whether the collateral settlement instructions are automated or not, it is important that a record is kept of them, and that settlements are instructed or approved by someone within the firm with a satisfactory level of authority.

A NOTE ON CREATING INSTRUCTIONS
FOR COLLATERAL MOVEMENTS

There are two predominant business models in use for the sourcing and investment of collateral assets. The first, and most straightforward, is where all collateral asset movements are managed through, and by, the repo or money markets desk. In this case, the

---

collateral manager will provide the repo desk with details on a daily basis, by an agreed time, of the expected incoming moves and the planned outgoing movements.

This model is employed by many of the smaller and medium-sized collateral management programmes. The second model, which is commonly used by firms with larger collateral management programmes, is where the collateral management team have a dedicated collateral account in which they keep incoming collateral assets, and from which they source outgoing collateral requirements. From time to time, the account is topped up by deliveries of assets from the repo desk, for which the collateral management team is generally charged a fee. The following note focuses on this second, more complex, business model.

In the event that the principal makes a demand for collateral, the principal must instruct its custodian to receive the securities 'free of payment'. The principal must issue an instruction naming the issue details of the asset, face amount and settlement date, and conversely the counterparty will instruct its custodian to 'deliver free of payment' the named securities, specifying the exact face amount and corresponding settlement date. The addition of 'free' to the instruction refers to the fact that securities will be moved, but no simultaneous payment of cash is required since the move relates to a margin call (that is, nobody is actually buying the assets). In the event that the assets are being returned to the principal, the principal must contact the business unit that sourced the collateral, such as the repo or liquidity desk, to determine whether they require the assets to be returned to them, for example for re-investment (that is, to close out a repo or loan transaction). They may prefer the assets to be retained by the collateral management unit as part of the general pool of available collateral assets for use in sourcing future collateral obligations.

Under this business model, if the appropriate lending business unit, for example the repo desk, confirms that they want the assets to be returned to them for re-investment, the principal's custodian must then be advised to instruct for two collateral movements. One set of instructions is required for the receipt of assets coming in from the counterparty into the managed collateral account, and another set is required to execute an internal transfer of the securities into the business unit's settlement account for same-day settlement. The counterparty's custodian would issue a straightforward 'deliver free' instruction into the principal's named account. If the business unit does not require the assets to be returned to them, only one set of instructions is required to receive the assets into the managed account.

In the scenario where the collateral assets are both returned to the principal, and additional collateral is delivered by the counterparty (due to a large mark-to-market swing through the neutral 'zero'), two separate 'receive free' instructions need to be made in order to channel the assets into the appropriate accounts. These accounts are typically the managed collateral account and the client's custodial account for safekeeping, or the account of pooled collateral which is available for rehypothecation.

In the event that the counterparty makes a demand for collateral, assets may be sourced from an existing pool of managed collateral or collateral which is eligible for re-use. If there is no available collateral, assets may be requested from the repo and/or the liquidity desk in order to source the obligation. In the former scenario, once the details have been agreed, both parties must instruct their custodians to arrange for the movement. The principal will instruct its custodian to deliver free the securities, naming the issue details, face amount and settlement date, and conversely the counterparty will instruct its custodian to 'receive free' the same securities, specifying the exact face amount and corresponding settlement date.

If securities or cash are borrowed internally, the principal's custodian must be advised to instruct for two collateral movements. One set of instructions is required for the receipt of assets coming from the finance desk's settlements department into the managed collateral account via an internal transfer. Another set of instructions is also needed to specify that the incoming assets must then be pledged out to the counterparty for same-day settlement. The counterparty's custodian only needs to instruct for the receipt of collateral from the principal.

In the event that assets are being returned to the counterparty, the principal will instruct its custodian to deliver free the securities, naming the issue details, face amount and settlement date, and conversely the counterparty will instruct its custodian to 'receive free' the named securities, specifying the exact face amount and corresponding settlement date.

Update records to show changes in collateral balances

Once the collateral movements have settled, the collateral management system or database needs to be updated to reflect the change in the collateral holdings. This needs to be done accurately, and on a timely basis, to ensure that the next collateral requirement calculation reflects the up-to-date collateral holdings.

As with the process of executing a collateral movement, the process of updating the records of collateral holdings can be automated using a direct custodial interface between the collateral management system and the custody system. Or, simply, the settlements area and the collateral management function can agree a controlled and efficient process for notifying the collateral manager of the change in collateral balances as a result of the settlements, and the collateral manager can then ensure that the collateral management system is updated.

Throughout the collateral management process, there are alternative automated or manual processes. Manual processes are perfectly acceptable if they are more efficient for an individual firm than automated processes and if they are as well controlled.

Reflect collateral holdings in credit risk management systems

As one of the primary drivers for the collateral management process is credit risk mitigation, it is important that the effects of taking and giving collateral are reflected in a firm's view of their credit risk and exposure vis-à-vis individual collateralised counterparties. There are a number of alternative methodologies for doing this and these will be addressed in Chapter 10, but here it is important to note that both collateral held and delivered should be acknow-ledged and recorded in the credit systems. Timeliness is again important, and while an automated feed of collateral balances into the credit risk system is ideal, a clear spreadsheet or e-mail will suffice.

The key information is:

a) the name or unique identifier of the counterparty

b) the amount of collateral delivered or received and

c) details of the unsecured threshold and minimum transfer amount.

Collateral risk management

We have mentioned previously that taking collateral is a risk transformation technique and that credit risk is swapped for other types of risk including legal, operating and collateral asset risk. This topic will also be addressed in detail in Chapter 12, but at this stage please note that the establishment of collateral agreements and the taking and receiving of collateral bring new risks to bear upon a firm, and they must be measured and managed.

Management reporting

Finally, the end-to-end process of collateral management gives rise to a whole series of information that is of interest to many different constituencies within a firm. This information should be tracked and reported on a regular basis. Examples of 'essential' management reports include:

■ The number of collateral agreements which have been signed; the geographic and sectoral distribution of those agreements

■ The amount of collateral held, and delivered, and received in total, and by counterparty

■ The amount of collateral held by asset type

■ The volume of collateral calls made

■ Special incidents including failures of collateral settlements.

Firms with robust collateral management technology can automate the production, and distribution, of these reports but for firms with a few agree-ments managed using a database or spreadsheet, they can just as easily be produced manually.

ALTERNATIVE CREDIT RISK MITIGATION TECHNIQUES

Although portfolio collateralisation is the most widely used credit risk mitigation technique in the OTC Derivatives markets, it is not suitable for use in every case. Chapter 3 looks at three alternative credit risk mitigation techniques to portfolio collateralisation with a brief review of the various advantages and disadvantages of each.

ELECTIVE TERMINATION RIGHTS

One of the most straightforward methods for managing the credit risk associated with a particular transaction is through the use of Elective Termination Rights (ETRs). ETRs are also be referred to as 'Unconditional Credit Puts'. These simple options limit the credit exposure of swap counterparties to an individual named transaction. An ETR works by giving one or both parties the right to terminate an individual transaction at an agreed date in the future. As with regular options, ETRs can be executed as European, Rolling European or American styles when it comes to the exercise dates. Note that the party that has the right to terminate a specific transaction is not obliged to do so.

As well as being linked to specific dates in the future, ETRs can also be linked to other triggers, for example, changes in credit ratings.

When an ETR is exercised, the contract is then immediately terminated and the deal is cash-settled at whichever side of the market was determined in the original trade confirmation. This will usually either be at mid-market or at the side of the market which is least favourable to the party which has had the Elective Termination Right available to it.

The documentation requirements for an ETR are very straightforward. ETRs can either be documented in the ISDA Master, which means that they apply to all the trades in the portfolio, or, if the ETR is to be applied to a specific trade, it would be documented in the individual trade confirmation.

ETRs are ideal for scenarios in which simplicity in credit risk mitigation is a key driver. In the case of a time-bound ETR, the only monitoring requirement is of exercise dates and this is frequently carried out by credit risk officers, obviating the need for a resource intensive collateral management infrastructure. With an ETR that is linked to a credit rating trigger, again credit risk officers are ideally placed to monitor rating changes. ETRs can also play a valuable role in circumstances where the use of portfolio collateralisation might be restricted, for example, because the counterparty has a negative pledge clause in their loan documentation which prevents them from delivering collateral under other agreements.

However, although ETRs seem like a sensible way of mitigating credit risk, they do have some disadvantages. First, predicting the optimum time to exercise the ETR which would be before the counterparty is at risk of defaulting against an exposure and generating a loss, but while they still have enough liquidity to make any payments associated with the termination of the deal, is difficult, if not impossible. Further, exercising an ETR can have a seriously damaging impact upon the relationship between two counterparties and unless the termination of the deal is by mutual agreement, this action would be likely to signal the end of that relationship. Because of the potentially damaging impact on the relationship, firms often have difficulty in deciding whether to exercise an ETR or not, and the view of the credit risk officer vis-à-vis the firm's exposure to the counterparty can be tempered by the views of the relationship manager.

And finally, for a firm to terminate trades with a counterparty which is in financial difficulties and adding to its liquidity pressures is not good for that firm's market reputation.

If there are large volumes of trades outstanding between two parties it is also operationally intensive to review them all and to close out the selected trades.

THIRD PARTY CREDIT SUPPORT

Another example of an alternative credit support mechanism, and the mechanism which has been in existence longest, is Third Party Credit Support. This method of support exists in two forms:

- A guarantee which is a contractual obligation by a third party (the guarantor) to make a financial payment if a prime obligor (the guaranteed party) defaults

- A Letter of Credit (LOC) which is a letter issued by a third party bank (usually for a fee) and which agrees to pay the beneficiary, that is, the principal bank in the case of the default by the bank's client or counterparty.

Both forms of credit support can be used alone and are simply documented under the ISDA Master Agreement. Further, both guarantees and LOCs can be used in conjunction with other credit risk mitigation techniques as a form of secondary credit enhancement, for example by accepting such assets as eligible collateral under the ISDA CSA.

The major benefit of using third party credit support as credit risk mitigation technique is the fact that it is very simple to operate. It carries virtually no cost for the secured party and requires little in terms of infrastructure investment. Third party credit support is easy to understand and, unlike Elective Termination Rights, covers an entire portfolio, not just single trades.

On the downside, a guarantor's credit has to be that much better than the party being guaranteed in order to be effective and acceptable to the secured party. Issuance fees can also be expensive, particularly in the case of a Letter of Credit. Further, the levels of credit support are fixed, and therefore usually end up greatly exceeding the actual portfolio exposure amount resulting in additional expense for the party who has arranged the LOC.

SINGLE SWAP MARK-TO-MARKETS

Single swap mark-to-markets or Resets are the most complex of the alternative credit risk reduction techniques to administer. The technique revolves around marking-to-market the swap valuation on agreed review dates, and if required, the out-of-the-money party delivers cash margin to the in-the-money party.

A swap transaction is typically executed at par (using current market rates) and so the net value of a trade is approximately zero at inception. Over time, changes in market rates cause the valuation to fluctuate, giving the trade some positive or negative market value. When a cash margin payment is made, the terms of the swap are amended, using the method determined at inception of the trade, and the cash payment effectively resets the value of the swap back to par, thereby removing the credit risk for the in-the-money party. The methods commonly used are 'Floating Principal Notional and Coupon Resets', 'Floating Notional Resets' and 'Fixed Rate Resets'. The technique is known as 'repricing' in the repo markets.

This technique has straightforward documentation requirements with the terms being included in each individual deal confirmation. Understandably, however, this method is time consuming to administer, and is not suitable for large volumes of transactions. Further, it is not suitable for all types of transaction and therefore does not address the credit risk of the entire portfolio in the same way as portfolio collateralisation.

CHAPTER 4

COLLATERALISATION OF REPURCHASE AND SECURITIES LENDING TRANSACTIONS

This chapter diverges from the OTC Derivatives markets to cover Repo (repo), Bond Borrow/Loan (BBL) and Stock Borrow/Loan (SBL) transactions. It provides a high-level review of the types of products that are traded within the securities lending market, while showing the impact that collateral management has on them. Although this book focuses on the OTC Derivatives markets, readers may wish to consider what impact, if any, the collateralisation of repo and securities lending transactions may have on collateral management functions focusing on the OTC Derivatives markets. Although the calculations used to generate the net exposure number for each trade may be different from some OTC Derivatives models, the basic process of monitoring the net exposure amounts and moving collateral to credit cover risk is fundamentally the same. This leads to a natural blending of support functions to maximise the utilisation of resources. Repo, BBL and SBL are, for the most part, distinct trading desks for many organisations. However, some larger banks have centralised the support for the collateral management of these products with OTC Derivatives transactions in one collateral management department. This has increased the potential for cross-business margining of securities lending and other derivative collateralised product types, and is a step on the road to 'enterprise-wide collateral management', potentially changing the way collateral management activities are performed.

This chapter covers three main topics: What are repo transactions; what are bond borrowing transactions; and what is stock borrow/loan? And importantly, how does collateralisation impact all three products?

KEY CONCEPTS

Before looking at the product types, we review some of the key concepts in the securities markets.

Delivery versus Payment as a settlement method

Delivery versus Payment (DVP) represents the release of an asset against the settlement of cash. The settlement process links both sides of a transaction such that both the cash and securities settle at the same time. The securities are released once the cash has been received and this generally occurs with automatic effect. The DVP process helps both parties to manage settlement risk, as the cash and security must be available for simultaneous settlement before the exchange can be completed.

Free of Payment as a settlement method

Where the trade does not involve cash at the point of exchange, such as with a Fee Borrow/Loan, the securities will settle Free of Payment (FOP). In this situation it is normal to have booked both the principal and collateral movements to occur on the same day. However, there is no guarantee that the exchange will be completed at the same time, generating a higher degree of settlement risk for both parties. The situation can occur where one party delivers securities, but fails to receive on the same day, leaving an exposure overnight or longer.

Delivery by Value as a settlement method

Delivery by Value (DBV) is a concept employed in the UK markets and is a term applied to both bond and equity settlement where trades are managed via CREST (CrestCo Ltd.). CREST is the multi-currency electronic settlement system for UK and Irish securities.

DBV is the delivery of an asset on an overnight return basis. It is valued at current market prices and usually settles on a DVP basis. The securities exchanged during the DBV process are taken from the CREST member's long bond or equity position, calculated from the remaining balance after the close of trading.

Settlement agents

In most cases, parties trading securities lending products employ a settlement agent, facilitating the movement of cash and assets. There are numerous settlement agents operating globally who are capable of managing this process, some of which have taken their services to the next level by offering collateral management expertise in the form of Tri-Party Services and Escrow Functions. These are typically three-way agreements where the agent acts as the intermediary, facilitating the collateral and trade settlements, while also calculating collateralised exposure amounts.

This next section looks at the individual trade types and the accompanying collateral management practices in more detail.

What is a repo transaction?

The word 'repo' is an abbreviation for a 'sale and repurchase agreement'. The repo market is an established global trading network accessed widely by financial institutions, fund managers and individuals of high net worth. A repo is classified as an OTC product as transactions are completed direct between the parties to the trade or through a broker as the intermediary. A transaction where securities are placed out in exchange for borrowing cash is called a repo or classic repo. Taking in securities in exchange for lending cash is called a reverse repo. Repo and reverse repo transactions are typically documented under a Global Master Repurchase Agreement (GMRA) as defined by the Public Securities Association/International Securities Market Association (PSA/ISMA), regional domestic agreements or bespoke agreements.

GENERAL COLLATERAL AND SPECIAL COLLATERAL

All repo or other financing trades will fall into one of two categories. The first is General Collateral. A dealer owns securities, and puts them out on repo in order to finance a firm's long position. A cash-rich institution reverses in securities and lends cash to the dealer at the repo rate. The institution may not care which specific securities they receive provided they are of acceptable quality (a criterion agreed between the dealer and the institution) and that the cash is fully collateralised. Hence this is called a *General Collateral* trade.

With a Special Collateral trade, a dealer is short of a specific security, which they do not have and reverses it in from an institution that does own it in order to settle the short sale, that is, to cover the obligation ready for the onward sale to another party. The institution delivers the security out against the borrowed cash at a rate usually below prevalent money market rates. Since the trade is driven by the need to borrow a specific security, it is known as a *Special Collateral* trade.

TERM REPO AND OPEN REPO

The duration of a repo transaction may vary from overnight out to one year, possibly even longer. However, given that the purpose of a repo trade is ultimately concerned with funding a firm's trading inventory, which may fluctuate daily, the duration of most trades is typically less than 3 months. Any trade with an agreed maturity is a term repo trade.

If either party is unsure of how long they want to borrow or lend securities, they may enter into an 'open' repo trade. In this instance, the trade is open-ended and may close out at a future date at the discretion of either party. This arrangement gives both sides greater flexibility and control over their position, but it may be more expensive to transact.

REPO TRANSACTIONS

The term 'repo' encompasses a number of different trade types and the major types are introduced in this section. All the trade types are made up from two elements: cash and securities. The cash may be any currency as agreed by both parties and the securities are typically fixed-income instruments issued by central governments, regional authorities and corporate institutions. Repo transactions are commonly transacted with G10-based issues (the UK, Germany, France, Italy, Belgium, the Netherlands, Sweden, Canada, Switzerland, Japan and the United States), emerging markets (Latin America, Africa, Eastern Europe) and even in higher risk corporate bonds known as 'credit repo'. The securities can be denominated in a variety of currencies and can be repo-ed against the same currency or a different currency, creating single currency or cross-currency repo transactions.

The next section outlines the major repo trade types. However, the name given to each trade type might vary dependent on the region in which it is traded.

REPO TRADE TYPES

The primary repo trade types are the classic repo (R) (Bonds loaned-cash borrowed, settlement DVP) and reverse repo (RR) (Bonds borrowed-cash loaned, settlement DVP).

Both R and RR trades represent the sale and repurchase of a specified security as assigned between two parties passing outright transfer of legal title. As an effective 'sale', the holder of the securities receives legal rights to re-use the assets for any purpose of their choosing until the repurchase date which is documentation specific. The repo rate applied under the transaction is fixed but can change with the consent of both parties. The trade may be confirmed as open with no end date, or a term basis with an agreed end date, and booked as either a single or a cross-currency trade. Any generated income (bond instruments can generate an income paid to the holder in the form of a coupon) paid to the taker during the life of the trade shall be returned to the giver of the securities following the payment of such income by the issuer. All R and RR type trades confirmed as a fixed rate R/RR should have supporting margin or collateral documentation in place.

BUY SELL BACKS AND SELL BUY BACKS

Both Buy Sell Backs (BS) (Bonds borrowed-cash loaned, settlement DVP) and Sell Buy Backs (SB) (Bonds loaned-cash borrowed, settlement DVP) represent the sale and repurchase agreement of a specified security between two parties passing outright transfer of legal title. This is documentation specific. The repo rate applied under the transaction is fixed but can change with both parties' consent. The trade is confirmed on a term basis with an agreed end date and booked as single or cross-currency. Any generated income or coupon payments which are paid to the taker during the life of the trade may be retained by the taker and offset against end cash flows at the termination date. It is common and acceptable to trade BS and SB without GMRA type documentation signed and in place. However, this restricts both parties' rights to make variation margin calls throughout the life of the trade.

FLOATING RATE REPO AND FLOATING RATE REVERSE REPO

A floating rate repo (bonds loaned, cash borrowed at variable repo rate, settlement DVP) and a floating rate reverse repo (bonds loaned, cash borrowed at variable repo rate, settlement DVP) have the same rules as classic repo and reverse repo with the exception that the repo rate applied under the transaction is linked to an agreed market source, for example EONIA, LIBOR or SONIA, and is subject to daily market fluctuations. The trade may be confirmed on an open or term basis and booked as single or cross-currency. Any generated income (coupon payments) paid to the taker during the life of the trade shall be returned to the giver of the securities following the payment of such income by the issuer. All trades confirmed as floating rate R/RR should have supporting collateral margin documentation in place. The market term for such trades is 'Pension Livrée', and they are commonly traded in the European market.

COLLATERAL MANAGEMENT WITHIN THE REPO MARKETS

There are two types of collateral involved when trading and managing a repo portfolio. This section looks at those different types and how they impact the trade and risk management of the portfolio.

INITIAL COLLATERAL

Initial collateral is agreed upfront at the time of trade and is locked in as part of that specific transaction. If the bond that is part of the trade is described as 'special', the cash acts as the initial collateral. If, on the other hand, the bond is 'general', the bond represents the initial collateral.

CHANGES TO THE INITIAL COLLATERAL

During the lifetime of the trade, both parties may agree to alter the structure of the original transaction. The two most common changes would be renegotiating the repo rate which is applied to the cash or renegotiating the security used as the collateral. These are examined in turn below.

A CHANGE OF REPO RATE OR 'RE-RATE'

In the example of classic repo/reverse repo or buy sell/sell buy fixed-rate transactions, the dealer will have agreed an initial repo rate for the cash on deposit from the settlement date start leg until the settlement date end. Over time, the market repo rate may change, in some cases significantly, requiring the applied rate on the trade to be altered in line with current levels. This is known as a re-rate. Re-rating will alter the rate of interest paid out on the cash deposit, effective from the new applied rate date until maturity. In this instance, no cash movements are made, as the end cash interest amount due after the effective rate change is paid net at the trade end leg settlement date. When the trade terminates, the interest to be paid is calculated using the average rate from the start date to maturity date.

SUBSTITUTION OF THE SECURITIES

If both parties have agreed that they have the right to substitute securities at the outset, it is possible to request a recall of the original security and to replace it with another of equivalent or greater value after giving an appropriate notice period. This may be the case where general collateral has been pledged, but over time becomes sought after for use in alternative trading opportunities, or 'goes special'.

CALCULATING THE INITIAL COLLATERAL REQUIREMENT

For any type of repo transaction, at the trade date the physical collateral to be pledged ideally equals the value of the cash or asset that is received at settlement date, leg one. In the case of a repo this is directly related, as the cash settlement amount is driven from an agreed trade price as a multiple of the nominal value. These concepts are examined further in the examples below.

Example

Party A and Party B agree the nominal bond amount of $10 million

The trade price is agreed at 85.00

Cash is exchanged on the start leg of the trade at $8.5 million against $10 million market value of the security

The market price for the security when the trade was agreed is 100.00.

In this case both parties have arranged to exchange cash ($8.5 million) and securities ($10 million market value) at a mutually agreed price (85.00). The price has been agreed by both parties, but does not reflect the true market value of the securities (100.00) at the point of trade. If that were the case, when this trade is marked-to-market an exposure of $1.5 million will occur due to the difference between the traded and market values.

This is a simple view of the relationship between cash and securities, but it does not reflect all that could have been agreed between the parties. If the dealers have agreed to apply a haircut to this transaction of 15 per cent, then the mark to market exposure will be reflected as being flat (0.00). The taker of the securities may have requested the haircut to cover either the expected market volatility of the asset or credit profile of the giver. In this case a price of 85.00 with a 15 per cent haircut, when applied to the bond market value of 100.00, gives a flat exposure.

COLLATERALISATION OF REPURCHASE AND
SECURITIES LENDING TRANSACTIONS

The market price of the bond is 100.00 with a haircut of 15 per cent. The internally booked value is 85.00. The bond/cash equivalent is shown as $8.5 million while the cash loan is $8.5 million.

CALCULATING THE EXPOSURE FOR REPO TRADES

The exposure for a repo trade can be defined as 'the value of the cash at settlement, leg one, plus any accrued interest to date, versus the net value of the securities at their current value'. This is examined in more detail below.

■ The value of the cash at settlement of leg one is the initial amount of cash which is transferred as part of the trade.

■ The interest accrued is a result of the rate of return on the start cash from the settlement date to today using an average trade repo rate.

■ The nominal amount is the physical booking amount of the bond.

■ The 'dirty price' is the current market value for the securities, which is equal to the clean price of those securities added to the coupon accrual, which is the fixed-income payment by the issuer, inclusive of any additional factors such as amortisation.

We now consider a further example which shows how one can calculate the net exposure amount of a repo transaction and to report which party, out of the two involved in a transaction, carries the exposure.

We consider a reverse repo transaction where Party A holds securities and has pledged cash to Party B at an agreed fixed rate of 3.00 per cent. The security and cash are denominated in USD, and calculated on a 360-day basis.

The trade nominal is	$50,000,000
The trade price, on a dirty basis, is	98.42
The repo rate is	3.00 per cent
The trade start date is	1 July 2001
The date today is	20 July 2001
The current dirty value of the security is	97.794026

What is the net exposure amount as at 20 July 2001 and which party is exposed to the other?

The answer can be derived as follows, using a reverse repo calculation model:

Today's date	20 Jul 01

(Bonds are held by Party A)

The nominal value of the security value	50,000,000.00
Bond Price (Clean)	96.34375
Bond Accrual (Coupon accrual to date)	1.450276
Dirty Price	97.794026
Current Bond value (USD)	48,897,013.00

(Cash is held by Party B)

Dirty Trade Price	**98.42**
Initial Cash Amount	49,210,000.00
Repo Rate – average for the period	3.00%
Accrual day count to today	19
Day count convention (for USD)	360
Accrued Interest to date	– 77,915.83
Current cash at risk USD	– 49,287,915.83
Net trade exposure in base currency	390,902.83

As the current value of the securities held by Party A is less than the cash at risk, it can be deduced that Party A is exposed by $390,902.83.

As this example shows, over time trades will generate an exposure, which is an amount which can be lost in the event of a default, due to changes in asset pricing and the accrual of interest to date. In such an instance it becomes necessary to apply collateral, or what is known in the repo and other markets as 'variation margin', to the trade as a protection against loss in such an event.

THE APPLICATION OF VARIATION MARGIN IN THE REPO MARKETS

Where market standards and documentation allow, it is possible to off-set the exposure of individual trades at a portfolio level. Trades based on different underlying securities, currencies and booking locations can be included. It is

Table 4.1 Variation margin in the repo markets

Trade	Base currency exposure	Calculation currency exposure
1	GBP 13,500	USD 20,000
2	EUR 10,000	USD 10,000
3	USD –20,000	USD –20,000
Net exposure	n/a	USD 10,000

typical for industry standard repo documentation to apply a calculation currency amount (Agreement 'base' currency) to each individual trade level exposure to enable representation in a standard currency. In Table 4.1 US dollars are used as the calculation currency. These principles are consistent with the practices used in the OTC Derivatives markets.

In Table 4.1, a net exposure of USD 10,000 is shown. Assuming the documentation which covers the trades permits it, variation margin equal to the net exposure amount can be called from the counterparty. In the securities markets, variation margin requirements are managed in three different ways: pledge or receive additional securities; pledge or receive additional cash; or re-price trades to new market levels. We will now look at each of these methods in turn.

PLEDGE OR RECEIVE ADDITIONAL SECURITIES

With respect to a repo portfolio, any securities which are held as collateral are reflected on a net basis against all the trades in the repo portfolio. In the event of a deficit in variation margin, it is typical market practice to pledge or receive additional securities which are of a similar or greater credit quality to those securities which are generating the greatest exposure within the portfolio. If the exposure is not clearly attributable to one particular security or transaction, it is customary to pledge or receive a variety of different securities as variation margin, often in different currencies, to offset the exposure profile which has been generated within the trading portfolio. Any such securities which are pledged or received as variation margin are generally booked on an open basis with the ability to recall, return or substitute the collateral daily, if the delivering party notifies the party holding the securities by a mutually agreed time (Table 4.2).

Table 4.2 Managing variation margin requirements by pledging or receiving additional securities

Trade	Base currency exposure	Calculation currency exposure
1	GBP 13,500	USD 20,000
2	EUR 10,000	USD 10,000
3	USD –20,000	USD –20,000
Collateral in the form of securities	USD –6,750	USD –10,000
Net exposure	n/a	USD 0.00

PLEDGE OR RECEIVE ADDITIONAL CASH

Any cash applied as variation margin is also applied on a net basis across the trades in the portfolio. The question as to whether cash margin is acceptable, and if particular currencies are acceptable, is documented in the legal agreement covering the repo portfolio. In the event that cash margin is pledged or received, it is standard market practice to apply an agreed rate of interest on any cash balance held daily. This interest may be capitalised and added to the collateral balance or returned to the pledgor of the cash deposit (Table 4.3).

RE-PRICING TRADES TO NEW MARKET LEVELS

Re-pricing a trade to the new market level is an early termination event, where individual trades within the portfolio creating the exposure are rebooked. If a

Table 4.3 Managing variation margin requirements by pledging or receiving additional cash

Trade	Base currency exposure	Calculation currency exposure
1	GBP 13,500	USD 20,000
2	EUR 10,000	USD 10,000
3	USD –20,000	USD –20,000
Cash collateral	USD –6,750	USD –10,000
Net exposure	n/a	USD 0.00

trade is re-booked, it will effectively rollover, keeping the original economic parameters of the trade such as the notional amount, repo rate, and the termination
date. However, it will be re-booked at a price that reflects current market levels.

In the example below, the original trade that gave rise to the exposure is
version 1, which is set to mature and be replaced by version 2, creating a flat
exposure. The termination of trade version 1 and the start of trade version 2
should occur at the same time. This will result in a net cash movement.

In Table 4.4 the portfolio of trades shows a net exposure of USD 10,000. Two
of the trades have offsetting exposure amounts of +20,000 and –20,000 that
create a net flat exposure. The third trade has generated an exposure of 10,000.
By re-pricing this one trade to current market levels, it becomes possible to
show a flat net exposure profile across the whole portfolio.

Both parties must agree which method of managing variation margin is to
be adopted. That choice is frequently driven by market practice with respect to
different trade types, although it is most common to use general collateral
bonds for variation margin purposes in the global repo markets.

Following this detailed review of the repo trade type, we move on to look at
bond borrowing and lending.

BOND BORROWING AND LENDING

As opposed to the case with repo trades, the institution lending the bonds does
not usually want to receive cash against them. The institution is cash-rich and
would only have to invest any further cash which was generated. Accordingly,
this transaction only occurs with special collateral. The dealer borrows the
special bonds and pledges securities of similar quality and value but which are
general collateral, building in a fee payable to the lending institution as an

Table 4.4 Managing variation margin by re-pricing a trade to new
market levels

Trade	Base currency exposure	Calculation currency exposure
1V1	GBP 13,500	USD 20,000
2V1*	EUR 10,000	USD 10,000
3V1	USD –20,000	USD –20,000
Net exposure	n/a	USD 10,000
2V2*	EUR 0	USD –20,000
Net exposure*	n/a	USD 0.00

* Repriced trade and net exposure

incentive to undertake the transaction. A bond borrow or loan is also known as a securities lending transaction.

Bond borrow or loans are governed under the following document types – Overseas Securities Lending Agreement (OSLA); International Securities Lenders' Association (ISLA); Gilt Edged Stock Lending Agreement (GESLA); Global Master Stock Lending Agreement (GMSLA); regional domestic agreements or bespoke agreements.

FEE BORROW AND FEE LOAN

We now go on to look at a fee borrow (FB), where bonds are borrowed against bond collateral and settled free of payment and a fee loan (FL) where bonds are loaned against bond collateral and settled free of payment.

Bond borrow/loan positions are generally booked on an open basis with maturity dates being eventually agreed by both parties. The borrowed bonds could be used to cover short trading positions on the repo desk or sold on through a cash bond desk. Whichever purpose the bonds are put to, it should be remembered that the securities or their proceeds would be returned to the lender at an agreed point in time.

Unlike a repo transaction where the cash and security are locked together under the same booked trade, the bonds borrowed and the securities given as initial collateral can be reflected as separate trade entries: sell (loan) and buy (receive). This allows for cross-collateralisation where single and multiple borrows may be netted against single or multiple bookings of collateral, creating trade baskets. An example is shown below.

Borrows (receive)   *Collateral (loan)*

Bond A $1 million

Bond B $1 million

Bond C $1 million

Bond X $3 million

The bonds borrowed are collateralised by bonds lent (see Figure 4.1). Both the FB and FL trades represent a loan agreement for a specified security between two parties, which, depending on the documentation used, results in an outright transfer of legal title.

The fee applied to each borrowed transaction is usually fixed, but it can change upon the consent of both parties, while the trade may be confirmed on

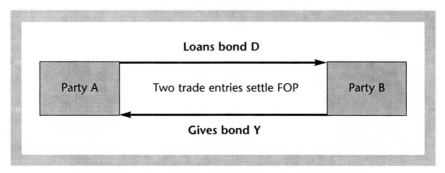

Figure 4.1 Fee borrow/fee loan vs bond collateral

a term or open basis. Any generated income (coupon payments) paid to the taker during the life of the trade shall be returned to the giver of the securities following the payment of such income by the issuer. The trades should be confirmed under the appropriate bond borrowing type margin documentation, for example, OSLA, GMSLA or GESLA. Variation margin requirements are typically covered with non-cash FOP general collateral. This variation margin will fluctuate over the lifetime of the trading portfolio, being re-paid at the close-out of the trades.

BOND BORROW AGAINST CASH AND BOND LOAN AGAINST CASH

This section looks at a bond borrow against cash (BBC), where bonds are borrowed against cash loaned with settlement DVP, and bond loan against cash (BLC), where bonds are loaned against cash borrowed with settlement DVP. The BBC and BLC trades have the same economics as repo but are documented as a borrow/loan transaction. The trades have a repo rate on the cash collateral delivered and a fee due to the giver, which is usually netted as one fee or rebate amount, taking into account the rate due on the cash collateral and the fee due on the securities borrowed. The trades should be confirmed under the appropriate bond borrowing collateral documentation.

In most cases, the re-pricing of trades which have given rise to an exposure will be the method of meeting ongoing variation margin requirements. This allows trades to be changed at the individual transaction level which is most suitable when an agent lender is required to collateralise its funds on a non-aggregate basis (see Figure 4.2).

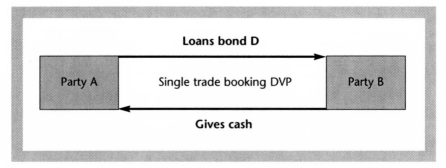

Figure 4.2 Bond borrow/loan vs cash collateral

SECURITY BORROW AND SECURITY LOAN

This next section reviews the security borrow (SB) where bonds are borrowed versus cash for settlement, collateralised with bonds versus cash DVP, and stock loan (SL), where bonds are loaned versus cash for settlement, collateralised with bonds versus cash DVP. In both cases, the bonds borrowed are collateralised by bonds lent. The cash is used to reduce settlement risk and should be of equal amounts in both trade bookings (Figure 4.3).

Both the SB and SL trades represent the loan agreement of a specified security between two parties resulting in the outright transfer of legal title. The fee applied to each borrowed transaction is usually fixed, but could change with both parties' consent, while the trade may be confirmed on a term or open basis. Any generated income (coupon payments) paid to the taker during the life of the trade shall be returned to the giver of the securities following the

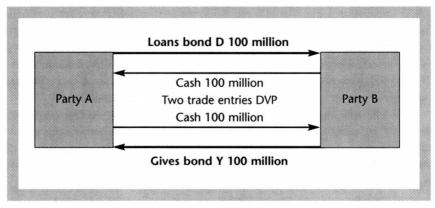

Figure 4.3 Bond borrow/loan (DVP) vs bond collateral (DVP)

payment of such income by the issuer. Trades are confirmed under the appropriate bond borrowing type collateral documentation.

Variation margin requirements are usually covered with non-cash FOP general collateral. Altering the notional of the bonds given and received requires an equal and opposite cash movement, to retain a balanced position throughout settlement

In this scenario, the bond borrowed is still to be collateralised by the bonds given, although to reduce settlement risk, the DVP settlement method is used. Figure 4.3 may resemble two repo trades, but in this case the cash does not carry a repo rate, as the transaction is purely fee driven. Bond D settles versus cash, then Bond Y settles versus the same cash amount. Any future returns in either stock are settled versus equal cash amounts.

The final section of this chapter reviews the stock borrow/loan transaction types.

WHAT IS STOCK BORROW/LOAN?

The borrowing and lending of equities is the central function behind the stock borrow/loan (SBL) business. Stock borrow/loan trades have many of the attributes of the repo and the BBL and also share many of the same market practices, as it is possible to borrow or lend equities against cash, equities or bonds, with the cash or the equity acting as the driver. As with BBL and repo, the borrow/loan of equities is fee and rebate based.

The stock/borrow loan transactions are governed under OSLAs, ISLAs, ESLAs, GMSLAs, regional domestic agreements and bespoke agreements.

BOOKING STRUCTURES FOR STOCK BORROW/LOAN TRANSACTIONS

Stock borrow/loan transactions are booked on an open or fixed-term basis with eventual maturity dates agreed by both parties. The borrowed equities could be used to cover proprietary short trading positions, be incorporated within matchbook trading or sold on through the cash equity desk. Whatever they are to be used for, it must be remembered that the securities will be returned to the giver at some agreed future point. Ultimately, all borrow/loan transactions will be closed out with the return of securities and collateral to the respective parties.

Stock borrow/loan trades and their associated collateral may be booked as two separate entries with the collateral in the form of cash or non-cash. This allows for cross-collateralisation where single and multiple borrows may be netted against single and multiple bookings of collateral, creating trade baskets. SBL trading requires both the taking of initial collateral and an ongoing variation margin process in much the same way as with repo and bond borrowing. However, in many cases, the job of the collateral manager is not only to manage the variation margin, but also the initial collateral.

Therefore, an SBL collateral management team will be involved in the following types of collateral management activity:

■ Initial cash, collateral

■ Initial non-cash collateral, variation non-cash collateral

■ Initial non-cash delivery by value (DBV), variation DBV

■ Cash marks: covers cash used for variation margining.

We look at these types of activity using an example.

A series of borrow trades are booked by the trading desk for settlement today.

Borrows

Stock A $1.0 million

Stock B £1.5 million

Stock C €1.0 million

The initial margin requirements for the three trades could be managed in the following ways by a collateral management team:

1. Initial cash
The collateral manager can deposit three cash amounts to cover the initial margin requirement for each trade in its base currency. The settlement of equity and cash can be done DVP or FOP. Settling DVP is considered more favourable in general, due to the reduction in settlement risk.

2. Initial non-cash
The collateral manager may deliver equities or fixed-income bonds. The party delivering the collateral will deposit a mutually agreed security of equal net value to the three borrows in the base currency as documented in the agreement.

3. Blend cash with non-cash
This is a combination of the two previous options above, where initial margin in the form of cash and securities is assigned to specified borrowed trades.

4. Blend defined stock and UK DBV-based equities

DBV can be applied to the GBP denominated stocks settling through CREST. A pool of collateral stocks, usually made up from FTSE 100 issues, can be delivered to collateralise the GBP trade on an overnight basis. The equity DBV collateral basket will usually settle DVP, helping to mitigate the settlement risk. Any remaining stocks could then be covered by alternative equity collateral.

This process will only have covered the initial margin requirements. For each day that these three trades remain open, the collateral manager will need to mark their value by applying the last close of business market price to the underlying trade in order to calculate how much exposure has arisen. Dependent upon pricing volatility and agreed thresholds, further variation margin calls will be required, when the initial collateral may be recalled, or a further combination delivered, depending on the net exposure. Additional variation margin may take the form of cash, equities (defined or DBV) or bonds.

The SBL process shares a number of similarities with bond borrowing and lending, one of which is the same documentation. Trading under the OSLA or GMSLA carries many of the same terms and conditions as if one were borrowing or lending bonds. Although many repo and bond borrow/loan trading and collateral management teams remain separate from the stock borrow loan business, growing synergies will mean that cross-netting and collateralisation of bonds and equities borrowed and lent becomes possible as stocks are given against bonds and vice versa. The issue may continue to remain whether the business and the market are willing or able to take full advantage of the agreements signed.

CHAPTER 5

COLLATERAL: LEGAL AND DOCUMENTATION ISSUES IN COLLATERAL MANAGEMENT

Lynn Shouls, Clifford Chance, LLP

INTRODUCTION

With the exponential growth of the derivatives markets since the late 1980s, market participants have sought to reduce increasing exposure under an ever-evolving range of transaction types through collateralised relationships with their counterparties. Collateral has also enabled institutions to transact with a wider range of counterparties than might have otherwise been possible, as well as to reduce credit and other risk. The benefits of collateralisation in the derivatives markets, particularly during the periods of extreme volatility in 1997 and 1998, are well documented: the general experience was that collateralisation of exposure significantly reduced, in many instances, the number and amounts of losses suffered.

WHY TAKE COLLATERAL?

Credit risk is the risk of a counterparty failing to fulfil its payment or delivery obligations for reasons relating to its ability to perform. The primary and most obvious reason for an institution to take collateral, is to increase its prospects of ensuring that obligations owed to it are fulfilled: upon a default by its counterparty, a collateral taker can, subject to certain constraints which are discussed below, use the collateral to satisfy the debt owed to it.

Other benefits might include:

▓ For regulated institutions, a reduction in regulatory capital requirements. By reducing exposure, collateralisation frees up capital to be used elsewhere.

▓ The efficient use of credit lines. If exposure to a counterparty is reduced through taking collateral, credit lines with that counterparty may be freed up for further trades.

▓ Widening the range of counterparties with which an institution may enter into trades. Without taking collateral, credit policy may not allow the entry into trades with weaker credits. With a wider range of counterparties comes not only greater potential for profit but also a diversification of risk.

▓ Better pricing. Taking effective collateral from a counterparty should reduce the credit risk associated with that counterparty and it follows that it may be possible to offer better pricing. A further corollary is that if a counterparty is offered more attractive pricing, it may itself be able to enter into further transactions, that is, trading activity may be increased.

VALUE OF COLLATERAL FOR DERIVATIVE TRANSACTIONS

Collateral held by an institution can be used to offset its exposure to its counterparty under a portfolio of derivative transactions entered into between them. This is because the collateral can be used, if the counterparty defaults, to fulfil the counterparty's payment or delivery obligations (with the excess, if any, of collateral to be returned to the counterparty to the extent not needed). Collateralising exposure under derivatives transactions with counterparties involves considerable day-to-day operational management because the aggregate value of collateral needed will change as the mark-to-market value of the transactions changes.

The liquidity of assets taken as collateral is important because they may need to be disposed of quickly, for example following a counterparty's default and before the value of the assets decreases significantly (especially as following a counterparty's default the collateral taker is unlikely to receive further collateral from that counterparty). Therefore the types of assets most frequently utilised in a collateralised relationship are highly rated government debt obligations and cash. In any event it is important to require collateral which is uncorrelated to the counterparty: for example when entering into a trading relationship with Company A, it is inadvisable to accept debt issued by Company A's subsidiary as collateral. If Company A defaults in its obligations to you, its subsidiaries are likely to be affected. The value of the collateral will fall and, when the collateral taker comes to dispose of it and use the proceeds to pay off Company A's obligations, it may well find that the proceeds are insufficient to pay off those obligations. This may seem obvious, but such proposals are not unheard of.

LEGAL STRUCTURES FOR COLLATERAL RELATIONSHIPS

Two principal types of legal technique are used in the OTC Derivatives market for the purposes of taking collateral. These are the 'security interest' structure and the 'outright transfer' structure. Although significantly different legal techniques, the objective in utilising either is consistent, namely the collateral-isation of exposure to a counterparty.

Security interest

Under this technique, the collateral giver grants a security interest, in favour of the collateral taker, in the collateral assets in order to secure its obligations to the collateral taker. While usually the collateral assets are delivered to the collateral taker (or its custodian), the collateral giver usually remains the owner of the collateral. The collateral taker's right is a property right in the collateral.

Upon a default by the collateral giver, the collateral taker has the right to enforce the security interest by (1) setting off cash collateral against obligations owed or (2) liquidating (selling) non-cash collateral assets and applying the proceeds to discharge amounts payable by the collateral giver.

This is the more traditional approach to taking collateral.

Outright transfer

In this technique, the collateral giver transfers full title to the collateral assets to the collateral taker. The collateral taker thus becomes the owner of the collateral. If the collateral giver fulfils its obligations, it will have a right to the 'return' of assets equivalent to the collateral assets which it delivered.

If there is an event of default in respect of the collateral giver, there is no return of equivalent collateral. Instead, the value of the collateral delivered is netted off against the sums owing to the collateral taker.

The outright transfer structure for collateral can work well in the invest-ment banking and securities markets where collateral is fungible so that the collateral giver is happy to receive back 'equivalent' assets. It will not be appropriate for non-fungible assets.

SIGNIFICANT ISSUES WITH THE SECURITY INTEREST APPROACH

The following issues should be among those considered when proposing to
enter into a 'security interest' collateral agreement with a counterparty.

Creation and perfection

The collateral taker's security interest in the collateral must be validly created
and properly perfected so that it can be effectively enforced, upon the collateral
giver's default, and afforded the expected priority over the counterparty's
liquidator and the counterparty's other creditors. Creation formalities are, under
many systems of law, relatively straightforward and often entail little more than
the due execution of a suitable agreement and delivery of the collateral.

It is, of course, necessary to ensure that the collateral giver has the capacity
and authority to grant a security interest. This due diligence can go beyond
merely reviewing the collateral giver's constitutive documents and the legal
regime within which it exists, as it may entail a consideration of other documentation, for example documentation containing negative pledges given by
the collateral giver, to establish whether the negative pledge prohibits the
creation of the security interest proposed.

Perfection of a security interest is often a rather complex matter. It is the
process by which formal validity of a newly created security interest is
achieved and, in many jurisdictions, is necessary to afford the collateral taker
the expected priority over others' interests. Examples of the steps necessary, in
different jurisdictions, to perfect a security interest include registration or
filing of details of the charge with a public official or in a public register;
notarisation of the document pursuant to which the security interest is created;
segregating the collateral assets in a special collateral account; notification to
other relevant party/ies; and taking possession of the collateral.

Which, if any, of these steps will be necessary to perfect a security interest
will depend on the type and location of the assets and the type and location of
the counterparty. In some jurisdictions creation and perfection steps may be
needed not just at the outset when collateral is first posted; they may also need
to be repeated on the posting of additional or 'top-up' collateral, or on the
substitution of collateral.

Enforcement

It is essential that an institution which receives collateral under a security
interest structure to cover a counterparty's obligations is comfortable that it

will be able effectively to enforce that security interest upon the counterparty's default. It is important also to have a thorough understanding of what steps, if any, must be taken before the security interest can be enforced and what delays, if any, may be encountered in the enforcement process.

For example, in many jurisdictions the immediate enforcement of a security interest may be prohibited by the imposition of a bankruptcy stay or freeze on proceedings that may be taken against an insolvent collateral giver; 'proceedings' here can include the enforcement of a security interest granted by the insolvent collateral giver.

So-called 'suspect periods' are, in many jurisdictions, also of concern, particularly in the derivatives markets where the need to collateralise fluctuating mark-to-market exposures may result in the taking of additional or 'top-up' collateral. A 'suspect period' is a period prior to a party's insolvency during which actions taken, which can include the delivery of collateral, may be at risk of challenge or 'claw back' by a liquidator or other insolvency practitioner, particularly if the collateral taker knew of the impending insolvency at the time of the relevant action, such as the taking of collateral. Suspect periods vary from jurisdiction to jurisdiction, but they can be lengthy.

Enforcement can also be made difficult in some jurisdictions because of the need to comply with procedural requirements prior to enforcement, and this can cause undesirable delay. Examples of such requirements include: the need to give prior notice to the defaulting counterparty that enforcement steps are going to be taken; the obtaining of a court order before the security interest can be enforced; or the requirement to sell the collateral assets through a public auction (rather than immediately on the open market).

It is plain, then, that in some jurisdictions the possible period of a stay or freeze, or the enforcement process, can be lengthy, and that obstacles to rapid enforcement may arise. It is important to acquaint oneself with the issues at the outset of a proposed new collateral relationship, as the potential difficulties may severely limit the otherwise perceived benefits of accepting collateral which is subject to only a security interest. Enquiry should be made of counsel in the jurisdictions of both the location of the assets and of the counterparty.

Rehypothecation

It is often regarded as highly desirable, from a commercial point of view, and often essential to the economics of a trading relationship, for a collateral taker to be able to put received collateral assets to use from the time of receipt to the time when they (or, more accurately, equivalent assets) must be 'returned' (more accurately, transferred) to the collateral giver. For example, the collateral taker might wish to use securities collateral provided by delivering it to a third party as collateral for the relationship between the collateral taker and the third party, for example where the transaction with the third party is a hedge for that transaction with the collateral giver. Absent the ability to use collateral in this way, the need to find new assets as collateral for the hedge might make it uneconomic for the collateral taker to enter in the relevant transaction with the collateral giver. For this to be possible, the collateral taker needs to be able to deal freely with the securities when it delivers them as collateral to the third party. Even though the technical legal term 'rehypothecation' has a specific narrow meaning, in the derivatives context the term is generally commercially used with this very wide meaning, that is, to mean a full, unrestricted use of collateral assets received.

In fact, many jurisdictions do not recognise the rehypothecation of assets received merely by way of security interest, and if the ability to rehypothecate is essential, then in such jurisdictions one would need to look to the outright transfer means of taking collateral (although as described below this is not necessarily a panacea for all). Currently, US laws do recognise, or allow, rehypothecation in the context of fungible securities, but the number of other jurisdiction which also allow this approach, is set to increase considerably with the implementation in the EU of the new Collateral Directive, whose terms require EU jurisdictions to recognise this approach.

Netting

Although, as will be seen below, the enforceability of close-out netting is a key component in the workability of an outright transfer collateral structure for derivatives transactions, it is also significant when proposing to take collateral by way of a security interest. If the value of collateral required to be delivered under a collateral agreement is calculated on the premise that close-out netting provisions will be enforceable in the collateral giver's insolvency, when in fact they are not enforceable, the collateral taker could find the insolvent counterparty's obligations significantly under-collateralised.

Where close-out netting is not enforceable, a possible solution is to require the collateral giver to post collateral calculated on a 'gross' basis (that is, collateral giver to post collateral in an amount equal to the aggregate of the collateral taker's exposures to it under each transaction, regardless of the collateral giver's exposures, if any, to the collateral taker under other transactions). However, such a proposal may well be commercially unattractive to a counterparty.

Taxes

Although more likely to raise issues in an outright transfer context, it is advisable to take tax advice when proposing to enter into a security interest collateral arrangement. Taxes could conceivably arise upon, among other things, the execution of the collateral agreement; upon transfers of collateral between the parties; upon the payment of interest (for example on cash collateral) or on the pass-through of coupons received on securities held.

SIGNIFICANT ISSUES WITH OUTRIGHT TRANSFER

As mentioned above, the outright transfer technique of collateralising exposure, and the ownership interest in the collateral which it conveys, is quite different from the security interest structure. It follows that, while there is some consistency of approach (particularly in the areas of determining the exposure of one counterparty to another, the value of collateral held and the corresponding quantification of collateral delivery obligations), different legal issues need to be considered when proposing to enter into an 'outright transfer' collateral agreement with a counterparty. Some of these issues are considered below.

Netting/'Enforcement'

In the derivatives markets, the two parties to a portfolio of transactions will often enter into a master agreement which will govern those transactions, will form the basis of the main contractual relationship between them and will, together with the trade by trade documentation relating to each transaction, form a single relationship between the parties.

Any master agreement can be expected to contain close-out netting provisions. Put simply, close-out netting provisions will generally provide for (i) a right (on the part of the non-defaulting party) of early termination of all transactions entered into between the parties on the default (including, in particular, the occurrence of an insolvency event) of either of them and (ii) the calculation of a single net payment amount to be made by one party to the other on such early termination.

The importance of the enforceability of close-out netting provisions is not, of course, limited to collateralised relationships: on the insolvent default of one party, the other would not wish to find itself being required by a liquidator to make payment under transactions where the insolvent counterparty was 'in-the-money', yet at risk of non-payment by the counterparty under transactions where the counterparty is 'out-of-the-money'. Close-out netting arrangements are adopted with the aim of avoiding such a problem.

The use of an outright transfer approach to collateralise the obligations of the parties to derivative transactions introduces another element to the close-out netting provisions and calculations. Upon an early termination, the value of collateral delivered to the collateral taker will be deemed an amount owed to the collateral giver, and this amount will form part of the calculation of the single net sum to be paid by one party to the other (as described above).

This is the means by which the collateral taker's rights under an outright transfer collateral agreement are 'enforced'. This explains why the enforceability of the close-out netting provisions is fundamental to a decision to use this collateral technique.

It is important to remember that, even if one has taken advice on the effectiveness of netting in a particular context, it is necessary to ensure that the inclusion of the value of collateral in a close-out netting calculation will be enforceable. This is not so in all jurisdictions, even those where close-out netting of transaction exposures would be enforceable, and in such jurisdictions (as well as those in which close-out netting may not be enforceable at all), use of an outright transfer collateral agreement is not really a viable option.

Recharacterisation

'Perfection' is not in itself an issue when taking collateral by way of outright transfer, because the collateral taker is supposed to get full title to, and rights in, collateral received.

However, it is necessary to take advice on how to achieve an effective transfer of title to the collateral assets and on the risk of the transfer of title being recharacterised as a security interest. The most obvious consequence of a purported outright transfer being recharacterised as a security interest, is that the collateral taker may find itself with merely a security interest in the collateral assets. Thinking that it has received full title to the assets, the collateral taker is unlikely to have taken any necessary perfection steps and therefore, if any are required, will probably not have the expected priority over other creditors and a liquidator of the counterparty.

How to achieve an effective outright transfer of collateral is a question for counsel in the jurisdiction of the location of the assets. The question of where an asset is located is a sometimes difficult one and is considered further below.

The likelihood of an outright transfer being recharactersied is a question for counsel in the jurisdictions of (i) the collateral giver, (ii) the location of the assets, and (iii) the governing law of the outright transfer collateral agreement.

Suspect periods

The comments made above regarding suspect periods are equally applicable to transfers of collateral under an outright transfer collateral agreement. In other words, the collateral taker should investigate whether its counterparty (or its counterparty's liquidator) will be able to recover any transfers of collateral made during a 'suspect period' prior to the onset of insolvency.

Overcollateralisation

One particular issue with the outright transfer technique is that of a party delivering too much collateral (or the collateral value to mark-to-market exposure ratio increasing so that collateral held should be returned). This is because ownership will have been transferred in full, rather than a mere security interest have been granted. In these instances, the party which has posted the collateral has credit risk on the other party for the return of excess posted collateral.

Rehypothecation

The limitations which are to be found in many jurisdictions on the ability to rehypothecate collateral assets received are not an issue for a collateral taker to which full title to collateral assets has been transferred. If the collateral taker has full title to assets, it follows that, if it has not granted any other interest in them, it can effectively do with them as it likes.

Provided that it will be appropriate to use an outright transfer collateral agreement, the ability to rehypothecate assets received will make such an agreement a commercially attractive proposition.

Taxes

While tax considerations will, of course, vary from jurisdiction to jurisdiction, they are more likely to be significant in relation to outright transfer collateral agreement because tax liabilities often 'follow' transfer of title. Accordingly, tax advice will need to be taken.

SECURITY INTEREST VERSUS OUTRIGHT TRANSFER – WHICH TO USE?

When determining the preferred legal approach (whether security interest or outright transfer) to taking collateral from a counterparty, three key questions should be considered. These are (1) what is the nature of the collateral? (2) in which jurisdiction is the collateral located? and (3) in which jurisdiction is the counterparty incorporated or established?

Why are these questions so key? Taking the questions in turn:

What is the collateral?

How interests in assets are created, transferred, perfected and enforced depends on the nature and location of the collateral. For example, as a matter of English law:

- bearer bonds are transferred by delivery
- contractual rights are transferred by assignment (whether by way of security or otherwise)
- book-entry securities are transferred by the giving of instructions to the relevant depository institution
- security interest in a book debt (for example, debt claim representing 'cash') given by an English company is perfected by registration.

Where is the collateral located?

Where the collateral is located is probably the most important of the three questions, because most countries' conflicts of laws rules look to the law of the jurisdiction of the location of the assets (the assets' *lex situs*) to determine such issues as (1) how a security interest in those assets is created, (2) how the security interest is perfected, (3) whether those assets may be 'rehypothecated' in the 'full' sense, and (4) how to effect an outright transfer of the assets.

Where the collateral is located is in itself an interesting and sometimes difficult question, particularly in the case of, for example, securities held in a clearing system through a series of intermediaries. There is current important debate on this issue; please see 'Recent legal developments – in brief' below.

Where are the parties located?

The location of the counterparty becomes of particular interest upon that party's insolvency:

1. As the insolvency rules of a party's jurisdiction of incorporation or estab-lishment are likely to be the most relevant such rules on its insolvency, it is important to consider whether, in that jurisdiction, close-out netting will be enforceable.

2. What are the rules in the counterparty's jurisdiction regarding enforcement against an insolvent party? Is there a 'suspect' period prior to insolvency, such that transactions entered into by a party during that period would be voidable by a liquidator or unenforceable? Are there freezes or stays on enforcement? These issues are considered more fully above.

3. What are the registration requirements in the jurisdiction of the location of the counterparty? For example, if an English company creates a charge over a 'book debt', particulars of that charge should be delivered to the Companies Registrar within 21 days of its creation. If particulars are not so delivered, the charge will be void against a liquidator and any creditor of the company.

Furthermore:

1. Recharacterisation risk must be analysed in the jurisdiction of the counterparty.

2. Tax issues. Are withholding taxes applicable to payments of interest on cash collateral? Should stamp or other duties be paid on execution of the collat-eral agreement or transfers of collateral?

3. Other formalities. For example, some jurisdictions require that contracts be created in a particular language in order that they be enforceable. Special execution formalities might apply.

The answers to all of the above, and other, questions will be relevant to the choice of the collateral structure to be used, that is, whether security interest or outright transfer. While as a rule of thumb one might conclude that if the right to rehypothecate is an essential feature of the relationship the outright transfer structure would be commercially more attractive, it should always be borne in mind that the suitability of the mechanism depends on the enforceability of close-out netting provisions in the jurisdiction of both parties. Thus, if a coun-terparty is located in a jurisdiction which is 'hostile' to close-out netting, the parties' choice will be limited to the security interest route (and of course other credit enhancement techniques). It is unfortunately the case that sometimes no perfect solution can be found.

ISDA COLLATERAL DOCUMENTATION

The current suite of collateral documentation published by the International Swaps and Derivatives Association, Inc. ('ISDA®') comprises primarily the following: the ISDA New York law Credit Support Annex (security interest); the ISDA English law Credit Support Deed (security interest) (infrequently used); the ISDA English law Credit Support Annex (outright transfer); the ISDA Japanese law Credit Support Annex (security interest and 'lending collateral' provisions); and the 2001 ISDA Margin Provisions.

The ISDA New York law security interest and the ISDA English law outright transfer forms are currently the most widely used and have the features described in the earlier part of this chapter. There are several obvious advantages in using industry 'standard' documentation:

■ familiarity with documentation reduces negotiation time and expense

■ mechanisms and concepts common to all forms (for example, calculations of collateral delivery obligations) facilitate understanding

■ members of an industry association (here, ISDA) are entitled to rely on netting and collateral opinions, prepared for the association, on that association's 'standard' documentation.

The 2001 ISDA Margin Provisions, published by ISDA, consolidate and simplify the existing suite of ISDA credit support documents. The main objectives of the Margin Provisions are to: simplify the documentation architecture; combine different jurisdiction-specific approaches to taking collateral within the framework of one document; make the language used more 'plain English'; tighten the timeframes involved in the collateral process (for example delivery, substitution, disputes) in order to reduce credit risk; and address some previously unaddressed aspects of current market practice.

At the time of writing the Margin Provisions await broad market acceptance.

RECENT LEGAL DEVELOPMENTS – IN BRIEF

There has been a number of recent developments which are likely to be relevant, to a greater or lesser extent, to the often complex area of cross-border collateralisation. These developments include the EU Insolvency Regulation

('EUIR'), the Winding up Directive for Insurance Undertakings ('WD(I)') and the Winding up Directive for Credit Institutions ('WD(C)').

The EUIR came into force directly (without the need for implementing legislation) in all EU Member States (except Denmark) on 31 May 2002. It applies to corporates, partnerships and individuals but not to banks, insurers, funds or investment firms which take client money or assets. The WD(I) applies to insurers and must be implemented by EU Member States by 20 April 2003. The WD(C) applies to banks and building societies and must be implemented by EU Member States by 5 May 2004.

By and large, the new measures do not affect the substance of Member States' insolvency laws, but rather set out the rules for determining which system of insolvency law applies. The importance of understanding what will happen to collateral arrangements on a counterparty's insolvency is highlighted in several places above.

The central theme of all three new measures is that Home State law governs the effects of insolvency proceedings across the EU. However, in the case of, for example, property rights (such as rights under a security interest granted over collateral assets) and set-off rights, Home State insolvency law is disapplied.

There are some important differences between the three new measures, but probably the most significant is that under only the EUIR can Member States, other than the Home State, open insolvency proceedings, too, if assets of the bankrupt entity are located in that Member State. Thus it is again important to know where assets are located. As mentioned above, this is a difficult area but the EUIR adopts the rule that unregistered assets which are 'claims' against third parties (such as 'cash at bank', debts and receivables, and so forth) are located in the place where the obligor (the obligor of 'cash at bank' is that bank) has its head office. This is an important development and should be considered when needing to perfect collateral arrangements in respect of any such receivables, cash and the like.

As for set-off, all three legislative measures state that insolvency proceedings cannot affect a right of set-off provided that it is effective under the law governing the insolvent party's claim.

EU COLLATERAL DIRECTIVE

The EU Collateral Directive is intended to be implemented by EU Member States by 27 December 2003. Its purpose is to cut through layers of different and sometimes archaic laws relevant to taking collateral which are currently to be found across the Member States' jurisdictions, thus unifying, as far as possible, the approach to taking collateral across the EU. Briefly put, the Directive requires Member States to abolish most of their legal rules regarding the

creation, perfection and enforcement of rights in collateral, rendering each of
these processes much simpler than before. Even some insolvency rules, which
currently allow insolvency officials to claw back collateral provided at the
moment that insolvency proceedings are initiated, must be repealed. Outright
transfer of title to collateral must no longer be recharacterised, close-out
netting arrangements must be recognised and rehypothecation of collateral is
to be permitted.

Thus most of the significant issues which are described in relation to taking
collateral by way of either security interests or outright transfer of title will fall
away for collateral arrangements between parties in the categories set out in
the Directive (which include, in brief, public authorities, central banks and
financial institutions subject to prudential supervision).

THE HAGUE CONVENTION

The purpose of the Hague Conference on Private International Law is to
achieve a common framework, agreed internationally and adopted in as many
countries as possible, for determining where securities are located. The location of securities is typically difficult to determine as they rarely exist in
tangible form and are often held through chains of intermediaries. It is important to settle the question of how to determine the location of securities
because legal questions relating to entitlement to interests in securities tend to
be referred to that location. In brief, the draft Hague Convention proposes that
the law of the location of securities (meaning shares, bonds or other financial
instruments or assets other than cash) will be determined by reference to the
law governing the account agreement between the account holder and the
relevant intermediary (the so called 'PRIMA' ('Place of the Relevant Intermediary Approach') approach). This approach is not without its difficulties
(for example, one has to identify the 'relevant intermediary', the account
agreement, and so forth).

At the time of writing a diplomatic session on the preliminary draft
Convention on indirectly held securities is taking place, and it is believed that
the proposals have attracted a wide following among OECD countries. The
Convention has been adopted as of December 2002, following which signatory
states will need to take action to ratify it.

AND FINALLY...

While collateralisation is the credit enhancement tool probably most widely
used in the derivatives markets, it is important to remember that it is only one

of several techniques which may be appropriate in any given situation. The use of other methods of risk reduction, including recouponing/repricing or elective termination rights (both transaction specific); third-party support such as guarantees and letters of credit; and insurance of risk or credit derivatives, should always be considered.

Furthermore, even following the implementation of successful collateral relationships, it is important that institutions remain abreast both of legal and regulatory developments and of how market and operational practice evolves. By way of example, the EUIR has had an impact on the deemed location of receivables and, accordingly, perfection requirements in relation to cash (and other) collateral may need to be revisited. As for market and operational practices, the advent and wider acceptance of the 2001 ISDA Margin Provisions may result in a growing implementation of shorter delivery and dispute timetables: institutions may not want to be left with outdated, slower, collateral processes and thereby find themselves at the 'end of the queue' if a counterparty starts to default generally.

CHAPTER 6

NETTING AND COLLATERAL MANAGEMENT

Credit risk management is achieved through a complex interaction of organisational structures, documentation, people, processes and technology. The appropriate technique for credit risk management will depend on the nature of the firm's aspirations and risk appetite for the complexity of its activities, and the technology choices available to it at the time. It is a certainty, however, that for any credit risk management technique, such as collateral management, to have any value, a firm needs to be able to take advantage of netting first.

Essentially, the ability to net under certain legal and regulatory conditions is the capacity of a firm to recognise not only its assets but also its liabilities when calculating its claim or debt from or to an insolvent counterparty and, therefore, when estimating its credit exposures to those of its counterparties with which it has signed bilateral master netting agreements, always providing of course that it has good clean legal opinions covering the relevant insolvency laws.

While the term 'netting' can be, and is, used in many contexts, there are basically two types of netting where traded financial products are concerned and the Basel Committee on Banking Supervision[7] has provided excellent definitions for them.

Settlement or payment netting is defined as the bilateral or multilateral netting of payment orders in a single currency on a given value date.

Pre-settlement or close-out netting is defined as the sum of the discounted present values of the unrealised gains and losses on all included transactions.

The difference between these two types of netting is that settlement or payment netting is an operational method of reducing the magnitude of foreign exchange payments in each currency (provided the two parties have previously signed a bilateral agreement to that effect), while pre-settlement or close-out netting describes the methods and calculations which may be used (provided the two parties have previously signed a bilateral agreement to that effect) to crystallise and calculate a debt or claim by the surviving party when the other party to the agreement becomes insolvent. It is only really at the point of insolvency that the two types of netting come together.

SETTLEMENT OR PAYMENT NETTING

Settlement risk exists because, in order to deliver on the due date the currencies they have sold, both parties to the transaction must pay away in advance of receipt of the currencies they have bought. The risk, of course, is that the currency you have purchased may never be received even though it has been bought and paid for in full. This problem is further exacerbated by the fact that the global trading day involves many different time zones, so it is quite possible that one party's business day begins many hours before the other party's business day.

A settlement netting agreement is designed to enable a bank to reduce the amounts it pays away to (or receives from) each counterparty in each currency. In most cases, therefore, it should also improve the liquidity available to the bank's treasury trading operation, and this benefit should be felt on a continuous basis as well as upon the insolvency of a banking counterparty.

The justification for the Basel definition being confined to foreign exchange is outlined at the beginning of a set of instructions and recommendations to regulators (Supervisory Guidance for Managing Settlement Risk in Foreign Exchange Transactions) issued by the Basel Committee [Basel Committee Publications No. 73 (September 2000)] and states that:

> settlement risk exists for any traded product but the size of the foreign exchange market makes FX transactions the greatest source of settlement risk for many market participants, involving daily exposures of tens of billions of dollars for the largest banks. Most significantly, for banks of any size, the amount at risk to even a single counterparty could in some cases exceed their capital.

All bank regulators are concerned ultimately about systemic risk and specifically 'the risk that the bankruptcy or failure of one participant (such as a bank or securities firm) will have knock-on effects leading to the bankruptcy of other participants, ultimately leading to a widespread crisis of the financial system' [EU Directive on settlement finality in payment and securities settlement systems, adopted 28 April 1998].

Over the years there have been a number of initiatives (FXnet, ECHO, Multinet, and so on) to reduce or eliminate FX settlement risk, the latest of which is CLS. Continuous Linked Settlement, which will be operated by CLS Bank International, is designed to overcome settlement risk as it currently exists. The method by which the system is expected to operate is known as Real Time Gross Settlement, and the intention is for CLS Bank to act as an 'honest broker' in a Payment versus Payment system (PVP) which will resemble the Delivery versus Payment (DVP) systems, such as Euroclear, for the securities markets. The central clearing house effectively promises not to release a payment to a counterparty until the receiving party has received the payment due from the counterparty. In the event that a counterparty fails to pay, the clearing house then returns the principal to the other party. Initially, however, only seven of the world's central banks will be linked to the system in real time, so very few currencies will be able to be settled this way. It is also likely to be a number of years before more than a handful of banks are operationally capable of linking to the system.

As part of their continuing effort to encourage banks to improve their risk management processes and systems, banking regulators have now acknowledged that payment and settlement risk should no longer be divorced from the pre-payment and close-out risk of the trade of which it is an integral part. In addition, the Financial Services Authority has confirmed that settlement risk will in the future be viewed as direct exposure to a counterparty which must be aggregated with the pre-settlement exposure. Depending upon how the regulators choose to enforce this, the requirement may have serious implications for banks with respect to their regulatory capital returns. As with pre-settlement or close-out netting, the Basel Committee's recommendations are likely to be enshrined in EU law. However, the revised Capital Adequacy Directive (CAD3) is unlikely to be adopted before the end of 2004 (CAD3 is not expected to be written until the end of 2003) and will probably allow a further grace period to enable banks to implement or upgrade their systems to take account of the requirements.

Worked examples

The following examples are provided as an illustration of the sort of issues raised. The first example is extended throughout the chapter:

Example I

Bank A has 3 trades due for settlement in 4 days' time between their organisation and their counterparty, Bank B (Table 6.1).

Table 6.1 Trades outstanding in Example I

Trade	Bank A	Amounts owing	Amounts owing	Bank B
1	New York	(Yen) 120	USD 120	Tokyo
2	London	(Euro) 100	(Yen) 100	London
3	London	USD 100	(Euro) 100	Beijing

Bank B is incorporated in Brussels and trades FX out of their head office and four foreign branches.

Bank A has a valid settlement netting agreement covering all their own and Bank B's branches out of which FX is traded.

What payments should be made and what are the risks?

Normal settlement netting calculation for Example I

Bank A sends net USD 20,000,000 equivalent in Yen today to their correspondent bank in Japan so that the Yen can settle.

The correspondent will transfer the Yen to Bank B's account at Bank B's correspondent bank in Tokyo banking hours on the due date (before 4.00am New York time).

Bank A would calculate that the Euro requires no payment from Bank B, and Bank A would wait for net USD 20,000,000 to be deposited in their account with their New York correspondent bank in New York banking hours on the due date (Table 6.2).

The risk is clear: Bank A may never receive the net USD 20,000,000 if Bank B is declared bankrupt in the intervening period. The benefits are also clear: Bank A did not have to pay away USD 320,000,000 equivalent in advance of receiving USD 320,000,000 equivalent (or not in the case of the bankruptcy of Bank B).

Table 6.2 Settlement netting in Example I

Trade	Bank A	Amounts owing	Amounts owing	Bank B
1	New York	(Yen) 120	USD 120	Tokyo
2	London	(Euro) 100	(Yen) 100	London
3	London	USD 100	(Euro) 100	Beijing

This is how settlement netting should, and in general does, work. Now let us look at what might happen when something goes wrong.

Example II

Two days have passed and there is now only one day to settlement. Bank A is informed by a Belgian liquidator that Bank B has been put into Receivership. The Belgian liquidator also tells Bank A that he has been informed by the Chinese liquidator of Bank B's Beijing branch that he will be dealing with all the Beijing assets separately and that netting does not apply in China.

Bank A quickly contacts their correspondent bank in Tokyo to try and withdraw the Yen payment but are told that it has just gone 'irrevocably'.[8]

How would Bank A calculate their claim for loss?

Settlement netting liquidation calculation for Example II

Trade 3 must now be dealt with separately.

Bank A has sent USD 20,000,000 worth of Yen and the Belgian liquidator may be happy to agree that he has dealt with his side of Trade 2. He may also agree, therefore, that Bank A has dealt with their side of Trade 1.

The Belgian liquidator admits he cannot pay his side of Trade 1.

Belgian liquidator may not acknowledge the net Euro zero payment because Trade 3 has been severed and he therefore insists that Bank A perform on their side of Trade 2.

The Chinese liquidator insists that Bank A must perform on their obligations under Trade 3 and send him USD 100,000,000, but informs Bank A that he cannot send their Euros.

Bank A will claim USD 320,000,000, of which USD 100 may be disallowed.

If the liquidator agrees the Yen net payment, Bank A's claim would consist of USD 120,000,000 for Trade 1, Euro 100,000,000 for Trade 2 (which may be disallowed even though Bank A had a valid settlement netting agreement and should not have had to pay this amount) and Euro 100,000,000 for Trade 3, that is, USD 320,000,000.

In this example Bank A's payments would consist of (Yen) 20,000,000 + (Euro) 100,000,000 + USD 100,000,000 and Bank A is likely to have their claim

Table 6.3 Settlement netting in Example II

Trade	Bank A	Amounts owing	Amounts owing	Branch B
1	New York	(Yen) 120	USD 120	Tokyo
2	London	(Euro) 100	(Yen) 100	London
3	London	USD 100	(Euro) 100	Beijing

agreed at this level and no higher, that is, USD 220,000,000 (or, to be more exact, USD 220,000,000 worth of Euros since a liquidation claim is invariably made in the currency of the country of incorporation of the insolvent counterparty). It is unlikely that any liquidator will allow Bank A to benefit by claiming more than they have lost or, in this example, paid.

So what went wrong? The fact that Bank B went bankrupt should not by itself have left Bank A in such a weak position. After all, one would surely have expected that Bank A's claim for loss would have been for a net total of USD 20,000,000m, whereas with no settlement netting agreement Bank A would have claimed USD 320,000,000, which is being the total of all expected receipts. Under Example II, however, Bank A would also have claimed USD 320,000,000 even though they had a valid settlement netting agreement. The problem, of course, was one of jurisdiction and the differing laws covering insolvency.

Jurisdiction and legal issues

A master netting agreement is a legal contract and, as such, should be enforceable under the governing law of its jurisdiction. However, when a company is insolvent, the insolvency law of the place of incorporation of a company will override the law of the agreement. In this event, trades transacted by the defaulting party and/or its branches may be disallowed or cherry-picked by the local liquidator if the local insolvency law does not allow of a right of termination and set-off.

The legal enforceability of the agreement, and therefore the ability to calculate the potential loss or payment due to, or from, a counterparty in the event of a default, is further complicated by the possibility of jurisdictional contamination. This may result when, even though the defaulting party is or was incorporated in a netting-friendly jurisdiction, the local liquidator of one of the defaulting party's branches disallows or cherry-picks those deals transacted by the branch. If the severance of even one transaction results in the invalidation of the whole netting agreement in the jurisdiction of incorporation of the counterparty, it will be necessary to exclude all branch jurisdictions with uncertain rights of set-off from that agreement.

Because of these and other concerns, it is imperative that legal opinions covering these issues be obtained prior to a firm's recognition of any of the benefits of netting – whether in terms of risk or capital reduction. This is not only the better and more prudent view, it is also a requirement of the FSA and the Basel Capital Accord. This requirement, and the time and expense involved in negotiating and reviewing a plethora of different netting agreements, has tended to encourage the market use of standard documentation and joint opinion gathering by industry bodies such as ISDA and ISMA.

PRE-SETTLEMENT OR CLOSE-OUT NETTING

Pre-settlement or close-out netting describes what happens with those trades which have not yet reached maturity or settlement when the insolvency of a counterparty occurs.

When the first Basel Capital Accord was signed in 1988, it became clear that the central banks and banking regulators in many countries were nervous of another credit-related melt-down of the variety experienced in the early 1980s with the Latin American debt crisis, and had every intention of trying to make sure that such an event did not recur. To that end they were keen to persuade banks to manage their risks more carefully and, if that meant persuading banks of the need to implement netting into their risk management frameworks, the regulators were not afraid of offering them an incentive to do so. For the first time in the history of bank regulation, the banks were offered a golden carrot. A regulatory capital benefit (that is, reduction) was available to be claimed if a bank could satisfy its regulator that it had put in place the systems and processes to do certain things.

To implement close-out netting it is necessary to assess all the legal, statutory, regulatory and credit implications. It is not sufficient, for instance, simply to sign as many master netting agreements as possible. In order to claim its regulatory capital netting benefit, a bank must also be able to demonstrate that it can 'manage its exposures on a net basis' and, in particular, 'that it has systems to monitor potential roll-off exposures'. [It should be noted, however, that the FSA does not define the exact meaning of either 'manage' or 'monitor' in its *Interim Prudential Sourcebook: Banks*.]

NETTING DECISION ISSUES

Under the global termination provisions of a master netting agreement, all transactions covered by the agreement are deemed to have been terminated simultaneously on the default or insolvency of a counterparty. All deals are marked to market (assessment of fair value) and translated into a single 'base' currency as defined in the agreement signed by the two parties to the trades. The total of all negative values is offset or 'netted' against the total of all positive values and this results in a single sum payable to, or by, a counterparty for all transactions.

The legal and jurisdictional issues already discussed mean that each trade must be tested separately for a number of different conditions before it can be pronounced nettable or not. The simplest method of marrying a trade up with its correct netting agreement would, of course, be to stamp the trade permanently at the time of its execution or confirmation with the unique identifier of the agreement until the termination of the trade or the master netting agreement. With this ability, the only tests remaining would be those pertaining to jurisdictional issues. However, documents are often renegotiated and altered without being terminated, laws change, banks merge or are taken over and trades are novated,[9] and it is therefore necessary to test all trades or 'open positions' for nettability on a regular basis.

In order to decide whether a particular transaction or product can be netted, and under which document it will fall, a bank must first know what documents it has signed and what attributes they possess. In addition, it will require complete, accurate and detailed trade data. Without both of these things, the bank will be in danger of including transactions which have been confirmed under non-nettable terms.

Certain types of transaction, for instance, are expressly excluded from some types of master netting agreement because in specific jurisdictions they do not fall within the list of product types covered by netting legislation. Securities, for instance, are expressly excluded from the International Deposit Netting Agreement (IDNA) even though the use of Certificates of Deposit are a standard feature of the money markets. Credit Derivatives, on the other hand, are excluded from some netting laws on the grounds that they resemble insurance products. Many of the countries, and jurisdictions, with codified law have excluded insurance from their netting definitions with the result that, even though you may have contracted a number of Credit Derivative trades with your counterparty using the International Swaps and Derivatives Association (ISDA) documentation and definitions to confirm them, those trades will not technically fall under the Master in the event of the default or insolvency of a counterparty incorporated in one of those jurisdictions. Clarity of definition of product type is therefore of crucial importance.

JURISDICTIONAL DETERMINATION

Having ascertained that there is a valid nettable document to cover a transaction, the credit system must make the following checks:

1. Is the jurisdiction of incorporation of the counterparty considered to be netting friendly? Does it matter, for instance, that many of the North American banks with head offices in New York are actually incorporated in Delaware for tax reasons? In the event of an insolvency, which state will appoint the senior liquidator and which state's law will prevail?

2. Is the jurisdiction of the booking office or branch of the counterparty considered to be netting friendly? What, actually and legally, constitutes a 'booking office'? Is it that the trader is physically located there, or is it that the system of record (that is, the books of the bank and therefore the assets) is physically located there, or is it that the profit and loss of the trader is booked in that country for tax reasons while the trader may be sitting in an office on the other side of the world? And just to complicate your decision further, does it matter for settlement netting that the trade was booked to Beijing but is being settled out of London?

3. Is the jurisdiction of the booking office/branch of your own institution considered to be netting friendly?

One has to apply the same questions to your own branch as those applied to your counterparty's branch.

RING FENCING OF JURISDICTIONS

The concept of ring fencing of jurisdictions, also known as 'clausing', is in effect a counterparty telling you that, in the event of a moratorium, or other economic disaster, affecting one of its foreign branches covered by the master netting agreement in question, you cannot look to head office to make good the debts of that branch. To put it bluntly, your counterparty is preparing to abandon its branch when the going gets tough.

In this case you have a number of choices. You can:

1. Sign the agreement and do nothing

2. Refuse to sign the agreement

3. Extract the branch from the agreement

4. Reciprocate by ring fencing one of your own 'clean' branches.

At the moment most banks seem to be selecting the fourth option. An example of this would be the case of Hong Kong. Since Hong Kong has a clean legal opinion, what decision will the bank make regarding any trade which their counterparty has booked in Hong Kong? They will not be able to rely on the global nettability of their document at exactly the time when they will wish to be able to, in this case because their counterparty probably still 'can' but is saying that it 'won't' pay, and even worse, the legal opinion may fail if the counterparty is not insolvent.

Many banks are vehemently opposed to the practice of ring fencing, believing it to be of dubious legality. So far there has been no guidance on this subject from either Basel or the regulators, other than from Hong Kong which has publicly denounced the practice.

The proposed new draft umbrella agreements, the Cross-Product Master Netting Agreement and the ISDA 2001 Bridge, which, for a number of reasons, are not yet in common use, may well encourage banks to sign bilateral netting agreements including only clean branches with no clausing because of the method of closing out the bilateral agreements covered by these 'umbrellas'.

All validity and jurisdictional checks must obtain positive answers for a transaction to be considered acceptable for regulatory/legal netting.

Worked examples

So, taking our previously worked example one stage further, let us see how a close-out master netting agreement affects the calculation for loss and, therefore, the risk.

Example III

As in Example II, Bank A has 3 trades due for settlement between them and the counterparty Bank B. Bank B is incorporated in Brussels and trades FX out of head office and 4 foreign branches.

This time, however, Bank A has an ISDA Master Netting Agreement with a Settlement Netting Annex covering FX for all of their own and Bank B's branches as included under the ISDA.

What is Bank A's claim for loss?

Settlement netting calculation for Example III

When the Belgian liquidator informs Bank A of the insolvency of Bank B, Bank A checks their systems to find out what their exposures are to this counterparty and find that, not only do they have 3 FX trades (as per Examples I and

Table 6.4 Close-out netting in Example III

Trade	Bank A Branch	Amounts owing	Amounts owing	Bank B
1	New York	(Yen) 120 ←——→	USD 120	Tokyo
2	London	(Euro) 100 ←——→	(Yen) 100	London
3	London	USD 100 ←——→	(Euro) 100	Beijing

II) in settlement, but they also have a number of exposures in the Capital Markets and Treasury areas. Trade 3 has been terminated and the Chinese liquidator has insisted on Bank A honouring their side of the trade (USD 100m) (Table 6.4).

The remaining two trades should then be translated into the base currency as documented in the ISDA Master and added as 'unpaid amounts' to the rest of the trades in the ISDA close-out netting calculation (in this example they net off to USD+20m as Bank A have already paid USD 20m).

Bank A's claim for the 3 FX trades would therefore be USD 120m of which USD 20m may be disallowed.

The fact that Bank A had a Settlement Netting Annex to the ISDA meant that Bank A had not sent payments for trades in advance of receipt except the net USD 20m of Yen. In this example, Trades 1 and 2 should net off completely under the ISDA Master and the liquidator may therefore disallow Bank A's claim of USD 20m. On the other hand, since payments should equal receipts in the foreign exchange market, it is also possible that the liquidator may acknowledge the claim since Bank A had a valid settlement netting agreement under which they performed in good faith. To date, there are no formal legal opinions available to the market covering issues specific to settlement netting.

Other than the addition of the ISDA Master, the situation in Example III is the same as in Example II. The vastly improved position on the insolvency of Bank B in Example III is therefore entirely due to the benefits provided by the capacity, under a close-out netting agreement, to collapse all values into a base currency and to net across all products covered by the master agreement.

ADDING COLLATERAL TO THE EQUATION

Since the mid-1980s when the first close-out netting agreements were being developed for the OTC Derivatives markets, banks have been keen to reduce yet further the risks associated with derivatives by collateralising the remaining net amount due from a counterparty when a close-out netting calculation has been made.

Just as in the securities lending markets (repo and stock borrowing), the collateral for OTC Derivatives is margined on a net basis and typically consists of either tradable securities or cash. The crucial difference between securities lending and collateral for OTC Derivatives is that repo and stock borrowing are collateralised businesses, that is, the collateral is an integral part of the structure and pricing of every transaction included under the master netting agreement, whereas the collateral given or taken under a derivatives master netting agreement rarely bears any relation to the trades or transactions whose net risk it is designed to mitigate. Collateral management is not a business itself. It is simply the word used to describe whatever the lender or credit provider asks for, or is prepared to accept, from the borrower or credit receiver as surety against the possibility that the borrower may fail to pay what is owed when due.

In the derivatives market where the rehypothecation or reuse of collateral is the norm, collateral can have the look and feel of a net pre-payment. Nevertheless it is not a pre-payment and, under the terms of the ISDA CSA and the master netting agreement (of which the annex is an integral part), the collateral held or posted is treated in default as if it were any other 'included transaction', that is, it is first marked-to-market and it is then collapsed to a single transaction which is offset (provided you have a clean legal opinion to that effect) against all other 'included transactions' under the master netting agreement.

APPLYING COLLATERAL TO A TRADING PORTFOLIO

If a bank cannot net for credit purposes, that is, manage its exposures on a net basis, it will not be able to apply collateral to those exposures in any logical or meaningful way. Under an ISDA CSA, or any other credit support annex, all trades included under the master are technically covered by the collateral held or posted – even in those cases where only a subset of trades have been used for the calculation of margin. This is because under the master netting agreement all transactions, including the collateral held or posted, collapse to a single transaction.

However, since one cannot net across non-nettable trades for legal, regulatory or credit purposes (that is, close-out netting) one cannot net across them for collateral purposes either. One has to net clean with clean, both trades and collateral, and leave the unclean, both trades and collateral, to be severed separately.

Essentially, there will be two potential future credit exposures – one for nettable trades and one for the non-nettable trades. How these two answers are aggregated for consolidation purposes is a matter of policy for each bank to decide. This decision will influence the choice of calculation method and the choice of functionality for a credit risk management system. If, for example, the closing-out of the nettable trades and the collateral would result in a negative exposure (or potential liability) while the closing-out of the non-nettable trades will always result in a positive exposure (or potential asset), it is likely that the bank will view the credit exposure under that limit at that point in time as consisting only of the potential asset.

The final example is provided as an illustration of some of the issues raised by the use of netting and collateral for OTC Derivatives.

Example IV

Bank A has 3 FX trades due for settlement between Bank A and their counterparty, Bank B. Bank B is incorporated in Belgium and trades FX out of head office and four foreign branches.

Bank A has an ISDA Master with a settlement netting annex covering all their own and Bank B's branches as included in the ISDA.

Bank A also has a bilateral credit support annex attached to the ISDA Master, but have decided to carve out all FX trades for the purposes of calculating margin calls.

Under the CSA, both Bank A and Bank B have unsecured thresholds of USD 20,000,000.

When the Belgian liquidator informs Bank A of the insolvency of Bank B he also tells them that the Chinese liquidator of the Beijing branch is severing all Beijing's assets and liabilities.

The liquidator reminds Bank A that credit derivatives are not eligible for netting in Belgium.

Bank A endeavours to find out what Bank A's exposures are to this counterparty and are told that:

3 FX trades are in settlement (as per examples I–III).

Bank A has posted USD 22,000,000 of US Treasuries as collateral for which they have a clean legal opinion.

The current market values under the ISDA Master for close-out netting are shown in Table 6.5.

How would Bank A calculate their claim for loss?

Bank A is likely to be asked to pay USD 155,000,000 (being all non-nettable payments plus the net negative difference of all nettable trades including collateral) and would claim USD 202,000,000 (Table 6.6).

Table 6.5 Close-out netting in Example IV

Trades	Nettable		Not nettable	
Interest rate derivatives	(–90+70)	–20m	(–20+10)	+10m
Credit derivatives			(–15+50)	+50m
Equity derivatives	(–75+25)	–50m	(–7+5)	+5m
Foreign exchange	(–60+100)	+40m	(–3+10)	+10m
Currency options	(–15+10)	–5m	(–10+20)	+20m
Totals		+35m		+95m

Table 6.6 Close-out netting for Example IV

Trades	Nettable		Not nettable	
Interest rate derivatives	(–90+70)	–20m	(–20+10)	+10m
Credit derivatives			(–15+50)	+50m
Equity derivatives	(–75+25)	–50m	(–7+5)	+5m
Foreign exchange	(–60+100)	+40m	(–3+10)	+10m
Currency options	(–15+10)	–5m	(–10+20)	+20m
Collateral posted	(+22)	+22m		
FX unpaid amounts	(–200+220)	+20m	(–100+100)	+100m
Sub-totals	(–440+447)	+7m	(–155+195)	+195m
	(–155+195)	+195m		
Totals	(–595+642)	+202m		

Without a master netting agreement, Bank A might well have been asked to pay USD 595,000,000 (all payments) and would have claimed for all expected receipts USD 642,000,000.

DID THE CREDIT SUPPORT ANNEX MITIGATE THE CREDIT RISKS?

In this example the answer is likely to be 'highly debatable'. In fact the CSA may actually have increased the risk because:

1. It excludes FX for the purposes of calculating margin calls

2. It includes all products confirmed under the ISDA (other than FX) for calculation purposes but credit derivatives are not nettable in Belgium

Table 6.7 Collateral call calculation excluding products

Interest rate derivatives	(−90+70)	−20m	nettable
	(−20+10)	−10m	not nettable
Credit derivatives	(−15+50)	+35m	not nettable
Equity derivatives	(−75+25)	−50m	nettable
	(−60+100)	+40m	not nettable
Currency options	(−15+10)	−5m	nettable
	(−10+20)	+10m	not nettable
Totals		**−42m**	

−42m (trades) +20m (threshold) = +22m (collateral posted)

3. It covers all trades under the ISDA and the ISDA covers netting unfriendly branches.

The collateral calculation as defined in the CSA (remember your collateral margin calculation takes no account of legal nettability) is shown in Table 6.7.

Now that we can see how Bank A came to post USD 22,000,000 of collateral, it might also be worth looking at what might have been the case if the Bank had negotiated its CSA with the possibility of the insolvency of its Bank B in mind. This is particularly important in a two-way, bilateral agreement.

Still using our worked example, Table 6.8 illustrates the collateral calculation following renegotiation of the ISDA and the CSA, to include all non-

Table 6.8 Inclusive collateral call calculation

Trades	Nettable		Not nettable	
Interest rate derivatives	(−90+70)	−20m	(−20+10)	+10m
Credit derivatives			(−15+50)	+50m
Equity derivatives	(−75+25)	−50m	(−7+5)	+5m
Foreign exchange	(−60+100)	+40m	(−3+10)	+10m
Currency options	(−15+10)	−5m	(−10+20)	+20m
Sub-totals		**−35m**		**+95m**
Collateral		+15m		
FX unpaid amounts	(−200+220)	+20m	(−100+100)	+100m
Totals		**0m**	**−155m**	**+195m**

−35m (trades) +20m (threshold = +15m (collateral posted)

nettable products and branches extracted from the ISDA and with no legally nettable products excluded from the CSA margin calculation.

With a margin calculation of –USD 35,000,000 and an unsecured threshold of USD 20,000,000, Bank A would only have been called for USD 15,000,000 of collateral, not USD 22,000,000. Therefore, the calculation of Bank A's claim for loss would have resulted in zero for the nettable trades rather than +USD 7,000,000, and while Bank A would still have been asked to pay USD 155,000,000 (being all non-nettable payments plus the net negative difference of all nettable trades) Bank A would only have had to claim and therefore possibly lose USD 195,000,000 as opposed to USD 202,000,000.

A collateral calculation under a CSA is not, of course, a liquidation claim. However, as a rough rule of thumb, the more closely the calculation under a CSA takes account of the legal requirements of liquidation and/or insolvency law, the more likely you are to achieve a genuine risk reduction. After all, collateral is only really useful if it works when you need it – in a default scenario.

On the face of it, this all sounds pretty simple, and indeed the legal principles behind the concept of netting certain specified assets and liabilities existing between two parties are reasonably clear. As usual, of course, the devil is in the detail or, to be more exact, the data.

THE IMPORTANCE OF DATA QUALITY

Netting and collateral both require accurate and complete data. Solving the problem of data quality ideally requires an almost bank-wide initiative. Each department or business area in a bank typically deals with the data it generates separately and tackles any problems it experiences independently from the rest of the bank. Users develop short cuts to meet their own immediate needs, and frequently ignore the maintenance of data which they themselves do not believe they require for the satisfactory completion of the tasks assigned to them. However, enterprise-wide data, both the collection and dissemination of it, requires not only accuracy but completeness and consistency. It also requires consensus, both as to its definition and its components.

PRODUCTS AND TRADES

It is quite common for a bank to have no central repository of product codes and those required for the market risk capital adequacy return are rarely maintained at a sufficiently granular level for netting and credit. Additionally, it is important that both the credit and the collateral management systems are able to recognise whether a particular netting agreement is capable of covering a particular trade.

It is essential that the structure and legal confirmation requirements of each product or trade are clearly understood in order to be able to define its type. However, it is quite common for the Front Office or Business Line to think of a particular structure as a single trade or product when, in fact, it is legally two trades and has been confirmed using two confirms which have been cross-referenced between two separate master netting agreements; for example, an ISDA and an IDNA for an exotic currency option based on a deposit. So, how does the system define a hybrid product? Is it a trade which requires one confirm based on two or more sets of ISDA definitions, or is it really a transaction comprising two separate trades?

Can a bank's trading systems provide the trade data a credit risk management system requires in order to make its decisions?

For example:

1. Does each trading system have the capacity to hold a trade linkage identifier?

2. If not, how will a credit risk management system find each leg of a trade that has been split? (for example, a cap and a floor instead of a collar)

3. And, even when it can, how will it know whether these two trades are indeed separate trades that form separate parts of a single-structured transaction, or whether they are really two 'stub' trades which have been shoe-horned onto the system for settlement purposes with the valuations running on spreadsheets elsewhere?

4. Some derivatives trading systems have a field to indicate whether a confirmation has been sent, but it is rare to find any data on a trade to indicate whether a confirmation has been received and, even more important, whether it has been signed and/or matched.

COUNTERPARTY MANAGEMENT

A credit risk management system will require a Counterparty Hierarchy Manager which is able to take account of multiple parentage (perhaps five companies, each owning 20% of a joint venture, and so on). In addition, it needs to be multi-entity, that is to say, it must be able to take account of all of a bank's own internal relationships, branches and subsidiaries.

Many banks sign netting documents with their own subsidiaries in order to reduce their connected exposures; indeed some are required to do so by their regulator. This, however, is somewhat academic if they have no idea of what those exposures are and this means that internal trades cannot be ignored.

You will require sufficient data on each trade for the credit system to be able to discern the difference between an internal trade booked between two trading desks of the same company, and an internal trade contracted between two companies within the group.

COUNTRIES AND JURISDICTIONS

Prior to the recognition of the legal right to net, all banks would have maintained a simple country table somewhere in the organisation for country risk and portfolio management purposes. This by itself is not sufficient for netting since it is quite common that a single country will have more than one legal jurisdiction – even the UK has four, and while three of them may be viewed as having essentially the same legal system, the fourth – Scotland – bears more resemblance to French law than to English.

On receipt of a new legal opinion concerning the right of termination and set-off in a particular jurisdiction, certain decisions must be taken and these decisions and the reasons for them should also be maintained in the system. Note that each legal opinion will pertain to a particular document type covering specific products under specific circumstances and written under a particular form of law.

The first, and in many cases the only, decision the bank must make is whether a legal jurisdiction is netting 'friendly' or 'unfriendly' both for legal/regulatory and for credit purposes. Most banks initially make a policy decision that the credit answer should be the same as the legal or regulatory answer. However, many banks have then discovered that there are a number of occasions where this decision is too inflexible for everyday use in the credit department, and that what they really want is the capability to override the legal answer for credit purposes – essentially a separate credit decision.

The obvious example of this is those EU jurisdictions which have not, or had not, changed or clarified their law as required under the Netting Directive. For legal and regulatory purposes the netting answer pretty much had to be 'No', but many credit officers believed that a liquidator in those countries would be unlikely to challenge a valid master netting agreement when his country itself was in contravention of EU law.

Some banks, however, wanted to be able to achieve an even more detailed answer than this since they believed that a liquidator might indeed achieve the right to cherry-pick his own nationals, that is, companies incorporated in his own country, but would be unlikely to cherry-pick the branch of a foreign bank, and in particular one whose own jurisdiction of incorporation was netting 'friendly'.

For a number of reasons, therefore, it is important to be able to make these decisions at whatever level of granularity is most efficient and which requires the least manual intervention, even if that means making it at the level of an individual branch in an individual document.

CONCLUSION

Close-out netting can provide the trading businesses of a bank with a hitherto unprecedented degree of risk reduction as well as providing a substantial financial contribution to the regulatory and economic capital costs of the bank's treasury and trading businesses. There are, for instance, banks with large trading operations who are able to reduce the regulatory capital they have been required to set aside for credit purposes by more than $1 billion per annum through their capacity to net.

The benefits to be obtained through the implementation of netting and the definition and collection of the data required are far-reaching in their effect. They extend well beyond the Credit Department and enable the bank to achieve:

- a more efficient use of economic capital
- a more efficient use of the balance sheet
- a reduction in the cost of regulatory capital
- an increased capacity to trade
- better pricing and performance measurement
- a reduction in the risk of credit loss
- an increase in the speed of credit decision
- better informed credit decisions
- improved data quality
- more accurate collateral calculations.

The use of collateral as a risk-reducing tool is, in general, a simple concept. However, just as with close-out netting, there are many pitfalls to establishing a sound position with respect to implementing collateral management to mitigate credit risk, and practitioners must guard against increasing it instead.

PART II

Collateral Management in Practice

CHAPTER 7

SETTING UP A COLLATERAL MANAGEMENT PROGRAMME

As more firms decide to embark upon collateral management programmes, so more people are charged with taking responsibility for this complex and challenging task. The people assigned to setting up collateral management business areas may not have any experience in this area at all, and yet they have to take responsibility for setting up, from scratch, an extremely complex function with many interactions with other areas of that firm. This chapter looks at the different steps involved in setting up a collateral management programme and provides some of the key considerations at each stage.

BUILDING A BUSINESS CASE

As collateral management has grown in popularity and stature, it is frequently seen as 'a good thing to do'. This steers many firms to embark on a programme without having fully considered the business case. The first stage for any well-run and properly thought out collateral management programme is to build a business case. The business case should cover:

■ Some background and introductory material on the use of collateral management in the OTC Derivatives markets for anyone in the firm who is not familiar with the area.

■ A summary of the key objectives of this particular collateral management programme. Every firm has different drivers, and these should help to mould the shape of the collateral management programme. For example, if the sole objective of a firm is to have a collateral management programme in place so that they can trade with supranational bodies or government agencies, the structure of their collateral management programme needs to be dramatically different from that in a firm which wants to collateralise its entire derivatives portfolio.

▨ A detailed review of the benefits, including accurate P&L impacts, to the firm that will arise from having a collateral management programme in place. This review of the benefits should include:

  ▨ reductions in credit line utilisations
  ▨ savings in regulatory capital
  ▨ reductions in credit reserves
  ▨ an estimate of the revenues expected from larger trading lines
  ▨ a prediction of the revenues which are expected to accrue from expanding the types of counterparties which a firm can trade with, for example hedge funds
  ▨ an estimate of the revenues that may flow from transacting different types of business, for example more exotic or longer-dated trades.

▨ A comprehensive breakdown of the additional resources which will be required to support the new collateral management programme. This includes people, capital and technology in both the direct collateral management area and all the ancillary functions including legal, credit, technology, market risk, finance and project management. The impact on other areas of the firm is rarely taken into account when assessing the true cost of a collateral management programme.

The business plan should be clear and easy to read with a comprehensive management summary. It should contain input from all the areas in the firm which are impacted by the advent of a new collateral management programme and should be signed off by them before being progressed through the firm.

Approval for the business plan should come from the most senior decision-making body in the organisation, for example the Treasury Executive Committee, to ensure that the decision to proceed with a collateral management programme has been definitively ratified by a body which carries power. This is indispensable in the event that a collateral manager meets organisational barriers to making progress during the process of setting up the collateral management programme.

DRAFTING A COLLATERAL MANAGEMENT POLICY

Once the business case to build a collateral management function has been approved, the next step is to prepare a policy document which prescribes how the collateral management programme will be run. Readers will find below a comprehensive summary of the areas which a collateral management policy should cover. Where specific groups of people are cited as having responsibility for approving exceptions to the policy going forward, it should also be assumed that the same group will have input into both the design and the sign-off of the policy (see Table 7.1).

Once the policy has been drafted and approved by the relevant body, it should be widely disseminated. Everyone in the organisation who will be affected by it should be introduced to the policy and it, and all subsequent changes, should be easily available, for example via the corporate Intranet. All exceptions to the policy, and the approving party, should also be recorded for audit purposes.

ORGANISATION STRUCTURE

When setting up a collateral management programme, the next key question is: 'Where will the collateral management team be situated from a functional perspective?' As we have seen, collateral management is a cross-functional activity and as a result, there are a number of different, and equally appropriate, organisational structures. Collateral management teams are most commonly located within an operational function, with the second most frequent set-up being within credit. Firms need to decide which is the most appropriate structure for them individually, but more importantly need to look at the different interactions and hand-offs between different parts of the firm and ensure that the processes and controls work smoothly and efficiently.

SECURING RESOURCES

The next step before embarking on the collateral management programme in earnest is to make sure that appropriate resources are available, including people, capital and technology. The resource requirements were outlined in the business plan and, as mentioned there, should take into account the knock-on effects on other areas of the organisation such as credit and legal as well as the immediate collateral management function.

Staffing the collateral management is a critical part of setting up a collateral management programme and should not be downplayed. Taking collateral

Table 7.1 Collateral management policy outline

Content	Approval for exceptions
Executive summary	
Statement of key policies	
1. Purpose and scope of policy	1. Head of credit risk management
State the purposes of the policy e.g. regulatory capital reductions; credit risk management reductions	
Expected benefits of taking collateral	
Legal entities and business included in the policy	
Products included or excluded	
Collateral agreements	
1. Use of collateral management agreements	1. Head of credit risk management
When will collateral agreements be used, for what types of counterparties?	
Which types of counterparties or business may be exempt?	
Legal issues	
1. Use of collateral agreements	1. Head of legal department
All collateral agreements should be documented in the form of industry standard or other appropriate documentation and should be recorded, and stored, securely	
2. Approved documentation forms	2. Head of legal documentation
A list of approved documentation forms e.g. ISDA 2001 Margin Provisions; French AFB	
3. Approved counterparty jurisdictions	3. Head of legal department
For example, collateral agreements with counterparties having New York as their jurisdiction of bankruptcy are approved, but those with counterparties having Russia as their jurisdiction of bankruptcy are not	
4. Title transfer agreements vs pledge forms	4. Head of legal department
Collateral agreement parameters	
1. Set parameters for collateral agreements	1. Credit officer/collateral manager
Who is responsible for setting different parameters which are included in collateral agreements e.g. thresholds and minimum transfer amounts?	
2. Determine which collateral is eligible for inclusion in collateral agreements	2. Credit officer for incoming collateral/ repo desk for outgoing collateral
3. Determination of the haircuts which will apply to the collateral	3. Market risk

Table 7.1 *continued*

Content	Approval for exceptions
Collateral agreement negotiation and set-up	
1. Determine who can negotiate collateral agreements	1. Head of legal department
2. Set time frames for negotiation	2. Head of credit risk management
3. Determine an acceptable time frame for setting up the collateral agreement and making the first collateral call once the agreement has been signed	3. Head of credit risk management
Monitoring collateral agreements	
1. Who is responsible for reviewing collateral agreements?	1. Head of credit risk management
2. How often will collateral agreements be reviewed?	2. Head of credit risk management
3. Under what circumstances can collateral calls be waived?	3. Head of credit risk management
Collateral asset management	
1. Determine responsibility for managing pools of collateral	1. Repo desk
Credit methodology	
1. Incorporate the benefits and risks of taking collateral in credit risk decisions	1. Head of credit risk management
2. Incorporate the benefits and risks of taking collateral into credit risk metrics	2. Head of credit risk management
Crisis management plan	
1. What happens in the event of a collateral crisis?	1. Head of collateral management
2. What are the positions on the collateral crisis committee and what and the responsibilities of those people?	2. Head of collateral management
Appendices	
1. Entities incorporated under the policy	
2. Included products	
3. Parameters matrix e.g. thresholds, independent amounts and minimum call amounts by credit rating	
4. Standard list of eligible collateral and haircuts	
5. Approved documentation forms	
6. Approved jurisdictions for collateralisation	
7. Glossary of terms	

mitigates credit risk, and organisations give benefit for the taking of collateral in their credit risk metrics. Therefore, it is imperative that a collateral management function is well run with the highest-calibre people. Good collateral managers are relatively few and far between and need to be sought out at the start.

The budgetary requirements will also have been agreed at the business-planning phase and should be allocated in full at the start of the programme. Again, a well-run collateral management programme is a critical part of a firm's credit risk management strategy and, while of course firms should concentrate carefully on cost control, unnecessary cutting of corners should be avoided.

Technology requirements are addressed in the next section.

COLLATERAL TECHNOLOGY

Once the business plan has been agreed, the collateral policy is in place and the appropriate resources have been secured, the next step is to address the firm's collateral technology requirements. Frequently, firms entering the collateral management arena jump straight to looking for a collateral management system, but the authors cannot stress enough how critical it is to have addressed the previous steps properly first.

Before a firm makes the decision to buy or build a collateral management system, they should first do full due diligence into the functional requirements that they have. An analysis of those requirements is covered in full in Chapter 8, but an excellent way of uncovering what is required of a collateral management system is to manage the first few collateral agreements a firm has using spreadsheets. The term 'spreadsheet' can bring connotations of a lack of operational control or inefficiency, but spreadsheets are an ideal way of managing a handful of collateral agreements. In addition to being a great way to prove the concepts, using spreadsheets is a most cost-effective way of managing 5, 10 or even 25 collateral agreements. Spending hundreds of thousands of pounds on collateral management technology may not be.

It may sound obvious, but after the appropriate collateral management technology solution has been chosen for a firm, it must then be implemented to best effect. This is addressed more in the next section and in Chapter 8, but on more than one occasion, major financial institutions have bought collateral management technology solutions and then never implemented them.

COLLATERAL MANAGEMENT BUSINESS PROCESSES

As mentioned previously, well-organised, well-controlled processes around collateral management activity are critical in order to realise the benefits of having a collateral management programme in place, or further to ensure that a firm's risk profile is not actually increased. This is also addressed in more detail later.

At the start of the collateral management programme, or after implementing new collateral management technology, the processes around it need to be mapped out, including documenting the people and groups that are involved at each stage. Once the process mapping of the current state is complete, the next step is to map out the target state for the organisation, that is, what the process flows would look like ideally. After that the firm should plan how they will migrate to the target state from the current state. Some of the key processes involved in collateral management are:

- Ensuring that signed collateral agreements are set up and margin calls are made as soon as possible

- Making sure that margin calls are accurate with all effective exposures to a client being captured

- Confirming that margin calls are settled on time.

Along the way, there should be a constant review of the key controls that should be in place to check that they are actually working. For example, does a collateral manager have the correct tools to ensure that all collateral calls that can be made are made on any given day?

Of equal importance to ensuring the requisite control environment is in place, is a review of the hand-offs between different groups and also a review to ensure that all the firm's reporting requirements are being met. For example, in terms of hand-offs, how does a collateral manager know that the legal department have signed and executed a new collateral agreement and start making collateral calls? And, in the case of reporting requirements, how do credit officers find out if collateralised clients have not met margin calls?

RISK MANAGEMENT

The final step in setting up a collateral management programme is for a firm to ensure that all the new risks that arise from setting up the collateral management programme are monitored, measured and managed appropriately. These risks include settlement risks, agreement structure risks and collateral asset risks and are addressed further in Chapter 12.

CHAPTER 8

THE USE OF TECHNOLOGY IN COLLATERAL MANAGEMENT

Technology is a key component in building a solid collateral management infrastructure. Larger, more mature participants in the collateralised OTC Derivatives markets have traditionally developed collateral management systems in-house, since no commercial vendor packages were available until a few years ago. Vendors realised this gap in the market, and have subsequently built systems that meet the needs of both larger and smaller collateral practitioners.

According to the 2001 Margin ISDA Survey, 63 per cent of collateral programmes rely upon a combination of several different technology platforms in order to support their business and technical requirements. These multiple-platform combinations include collateral systems developed in-house, spreadsheets, tactical databases and vendor packages. Clearly, and as highlighted in the survey, such fragmented platforms may lead to processing inefficiencies, data quality issues and audit concerns.

Meridien Research has predicted that spending on collateral management technology is expected to grow substantially in the next few years. While spending on dedicated collateral systems was approximately $54.4 million in 2000, Meridien estimates that spending could reach $134 million by 2005, with financial institutions in North America and Europe expected to be the biggest spenders.[10]

COLLATERAL MANAGEMENT TECHNOLOGY FUNCTIONALITY

A collateral management software application must support all aspects of the collateral management process, and should be robust, user-friendly, scaleable, and adaptable to individual business requirements. Firms investing in collateral management programmes are constantly seeking ways in which to optimise the efficiency of their collateral management processes, and the right collateral management software should help to achieve this, while ensuring a controlled operation environment. Combined with a best practice-based collateral policy, a collateral system will provide the foundation for an effective collateral management infrastructure, regardless of the size of the institution and of the number of collateral agreements in place.

In terms of more detailed technical requirements, a good collateral system should offer core functionality that should be considered as a minimum for even a basic collateral management programme. A collateral management application should:

- Provide support for the entire collateralisation process from start to finish

- Help to provide a secure operational environment

- Support industry standard ISDA documentation and also retain the flexibility to accommodate bespoke agreement structures and processes

- Perform the key calculations associated with the collateralisation process

- Integrate seamlessly with in-house risk management, custody and credit systems and processes

- Offer specific user privileges and audit tracking.

Although the margin call calculations can be broken down to relatively simple components, and can easily be performed on a spreadsheet, it is the convenience that a system can offer in terms of storing agreement terms, archiving margin call statements, reporting capabilities, speed and general audit and control facilities which are key benefits of having a more robust collateral management application.

Summary information would ordinarily prove sufficient for presenting a margin call amount to a counterparty, but as added protection against future reconciliation requirements and audit investigations, trade detail information (containing mark-to-market values and trade economics) and a complete collateral asset breakdown should also be available and archived within any collateral management system.

COLLATERAL TECHNOLOGY DATA REQUIREMENTS

In order to process daily margin call calculations, a collateral management application requires a considerable amount of information to be loaded on a daily basis.

Collateral management applications utilise the data which is provided to it, in order to determine whether each collateral agreement in the collateralised portfolio contains any margin deficits or excesses. The information is fed into the collateral system (ordinarily on a daily basis as part of an overnight batch), and is aggregated at agreement level. Data integrity checks should be made before the margin call computation begins, including whether all the feeds have been uploaded and whether the trade information is up to date. The margin calculations are then performed, enabling a single, segregated margin demand notice to be generated for each agreement, or constituent collateralised portfolio.

Depending upon the size of an institution's derivatives portfolio, some flexibility may be required to allow for varying degrees of automation when importing data from the various front office and risk management systems that supply the mark-to-market data. A derivatives portfolio typically consists of the following transactions, and separate data feeds may need to be generated for each product-specific system supplying data into any collateral management application:

- Interest Rate Swaps and Options

- Currency Swaps and Options

- FX Forwards and Options

- Commodity Swaps and Options

- Equity Swaps and Options

- Credit Default Swaps and Options

- Bond Options

- Repurchase Agreements.

It is recommended that any collateral management system provides for fully and semi-automated uploads of data as well as manual overrides. Users will need to be able to update trade mark-to-markets or asset holdings and prices in the absence of a daily feed or if a manual intra-day update is required. Since daily (and even intra-day) margin calls are the norm in the derivatives market, a high level of flexibility is essential to allow a firm to realistically achieve this level of valuation frequency.

A collateral system must also be able to integrate data from commercial applications and services, including market data sources to support asset pricing and credit rating contingent terms (for example Reuters) and credit ratings services (for example Moody's, Standard & Poor's), and settlement and custodial systems in collateral agreements. Alternatively, the application can be enabled to allow market data to be introduced into the system via manual inputs, which may be preferable for less dynamic data or collateral programmes with a few agreements only.

Seamless, automated data feeds, which may contain real-time mark-to-market updates (courtesy of superior trading and risk management systems), are a definite necessity in times of crisis, and could prevent an institution from losing money arising from unsecured exposure in the event a counterparty defaults on its payment obligations. However, the ability to quickly determine unsecured exposure and deliver a margin call notice to a client is reliant upon users often being able to manually update exposure and asset data upon a moment's notice in the absence of a data feed.

DATA FLOW OVERVIEW

The collateral management system aggregates the data and performs calculations based on the collateral agreement parameters in order to determine any margin deficits (unsecured exposures that requires a margin call) and excesses (any secured exposures that may require a return of collateral). The system generates individual margin call statements and call notices which are then distributed to clients (Table 8.1).

Table 8.1 Data inputs for a collateral management system

Data	Source
Exposure information: transaction mark-to-market data and trade economics	Internal risk management systems
Credit ratings data	Credit ratings services e.g. S&P, Moody's, Fitch/IBCA (and occasionally internal ratings data)
Collateral asset data and collateral positions	Custody and settlement systems
Collateral agreement terms	Legal repository
Market data: FX rates and asset prices	Bloomberg, Reuters
Instrument data: cash interest and coupon distribution data, stock record data	Bloomberg, Reuters

Management reporting capabilities enable users to generate reports across the entire spectrum of collateralised clients for cross-agreement analysis of a collateral portfolio, and net margin requirements across entities for firm-wide risk management reporting. *Archive facilities* store historical margin call statements and generated report results. In the event of portfolio discrepancies, data must be downloaded to a *reconciliation tool*, and any collateral management system should facilitate data extraction for these purposes. Pending deliveries and receipts of collateral are communicated to the custodian.

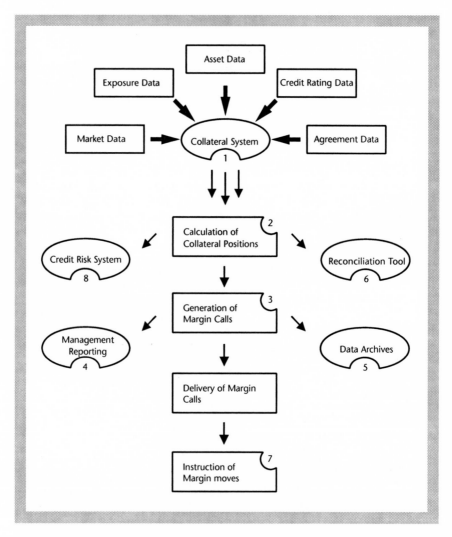

Figure 8.1 Information flows for collateral management technology

Collateral information (holdings and position data) is fed downstream into credit risk management systems for inclusion in credit risk calculations for corporate risk management purposes.

Figure 8.1 provides a summary of the various application interfaces that a typical collateral management solution requires, charting the flow of information and detailing system inputs and outputs.

COLLATERAL TECHNOLOGY FUNCTIONALITY REQUIREMENTS

A collateral system should support the entire collateralisation process. The next section reviews the main aspects of the collateral management process and takes a closer look at how technology is used to address the key business requirements.

CAPTURING COLLATERAL AGREEMENT INFORMATION

Once a collateral agreement has been drafted and signed by both parties, the terms must be loaded into the collateral management system. This process is usually supported in one of two ways: either through the use of an agreement input template, or automated transfer of terms. An input template should allow for the quick and easy transposition of collateral terms from the agreement into the system, guiding users through the entire input process and prompting extraction of data relevant to the collateral call process from the ISDA Master and CSA. Organisations currently using an in-house documentation repository system to capture the collateral agreement data will benefit from a data feed containing the relevant data necessary to support the collateral management process, thereby expediting the set-up process, limiting dual keying and minimising control errors.

Users may also need to record administrative information outside of the ordinary documentation terms which relate to an individual agreement, and so a collateral system should be designed to accommodate these to ensure the operationally sound management of individual relationships. Examples may include details of portfolio disputes, reminders and alerts (to check credit ratings and so on), incident reports (history of failed margin movements), counterparty contact details and general portfolio notes.

As previously discussed, most OTC Derivatives collateral management solutions are tailored towards relationships governed by ISDA documentation and all parameters contained within these agreements, widely recognised as the industry standard. However, in addition to managing the standard agreements, a collateral management system should also be able to accommodate bespoke collateral arrangements. A collateral management system should support the following agreement types as a minimum:

- 1994 New York Law CSA

- 1994 English Law CSA

- 2001 Margin Provisions

- Local law pledge or title transfer agreements.

Users should be able to select a variety of OTC Derivatives products, and define exactly which trades are to be collateralised under each agreement according to the documentation specifications. The ability to exclude certain product types and/or trades from the collateralised pool of trades is also critical in the event that such a provision is included within the documentation.

MANAGING THE DAILY CALL PROCESS

Since it is not uncommon for larger institutions to manage a portfolio of more than 2000 collateral agreements, measures must be put in place to ensure an orderly review process for the management of all margin requirements on a daily basis. Collateral management software should offer a diary management facility that provides institutions of all sizes with an at-a-glance overview of collateral agreements that require attention or some kind of manual intervention on a daily basis. Typically, diary management functionality alerts users to agreements that require a margin call on specific dates, and of any agreements with unsecured exposures arising from changes in market values or credit ratings, and also any agreements that may have excess collateral due to a reduction in exposure. Many institutions will rely on fully automated data to calculate margin requirements, and so a simple diary that lists all clients to be reviewed will suffice. Other clients may not have access to fully automated source systems, and so the diary will need to prompt any manual processes that need to be completed prior to the statement generations process.

The addition of workflow functionality that presents users with up-to-the-minute information regarding the current status of all collateralised clients and outstanding margin calls also features high up on the list of desirable functionality, and certainly makes for a more complete, fully automated system. User workflows prompt users through the various phases of the collateral movement process, tracking the status of all outstanding margin calls including the statement approval process, collateral in transit, and the settlement of collateral on a client-by-client basis.

GENERATION OF MARGIN CALL STATEMENTS

As previously established, collateral software must allow users to record the parameters from the credit support agreements, and to accept mark-to-market valuations of collateralised transactions from the underlying risk management systems, and valuations of any collateral assets from custodial systems. The application must then apply the rules of each collateral agreement to the individual collateralised portfolios and perform all calculations during the statement generation process. By incorporating exposure data, asset valuations and valuation 'haircuts', complex initial margin and 'lock-up' margin requirements, credit-rating contingent thresholds, minimum call and rounding amounts, the system determines whether there is an existing collateral deficit or excess for each agreement.

COLLATERAL CALL STATEMENT

A collateral management system must be able to generate margin call notifications and provide both summary and detailed portfolio reports in order to substantiate demands for margin. The summary reports must provide a clear, concise breakdown of exposure details, collateral asset valuations and any margin requirements, while detailed report pages should offer a comprehensive breakdown of underlying exposure and asset data. Trade detail pages should contain basic trade economics and mark-to-market data, as well as details of any unique trade level initial margin or 'lock-up' amounts. And asset detail pages should consolidate asset information at the agreement level to provide users with clear collateral position data and a useful itemisation of assets either pledged or received as collateral.

STATEMENT GENERATION AND DISTRIBUTION

Increasingly sophisticated channels of distribution are now employed by institutions for communicating margin requirements. While traditionally statements were delivered in the form of a faxed paper copy, more and more companies are turning to a variety of distribution channels for paperless notification of margin calls, including e-mail and use of the World Wide Web. Ideally, a collateral management system will support all of these methods.

PORTFOLIO RECONCILIATION

The move towards larger collateral programmes means that the ability to handle a high-volume portfolio reconciliation processes is imperative. The ISDA 2001 Margin Provisions specify a time frame for the resolution of any portfolio discrepancies that are identified between two parties. The new provisions stipulate that when a margin call recipient disputes a demand for either a return or delivery of collateral, it must transmit a notice of dispute by 1pm on the same day. The disputing party must then download and forward an electronic copy of their portfolio information (position and valuation data) in spreadsheet format to the calling party by 5pm that day, for review and reconciliation. Following a thorough review and reconciliation of the deal population and corresponding mark-to-market values with their own position data, the demanding party must then send notice of any discrepancies by 10am the next day.

Currently, most institution's efforts to reconcile trade portfolios are time-consuming and labour intensive. The process involves comparisons of spreadsheet files, sorting the data by trade parameters (product type, currency, notional and so on) and searching either manually or with the aid of an Excel macro to identify trade and valuation matches. After the positions have been paired, the user needs to perform a valuation comparison, the results of which can be used to isolate the cause of a dispute.

Functionality that allows historic reconciliation results (trade pairs) to be stored within a collateral management system will eliminate the need to repeat the pairing process for existing transactions should a future discrepancy arise. But valuation comparisons will still need to be made, and so a good reconciliation tool should allow for historic results to be archived to speed up future reconciliations with a counterparty.

Most collateral technology vendors offer reconciliation tools which may be used in conjunction with in-house collateral management systems or, alternatively, existing in-house collateral software. As a minimum, these usually comprise of a basic spreadsheet package that sorts and pairs the data. More sophisticated solutions do exist, and these consist of stand-alone, fully automated reconciliation tools that may be interfaced with any position management system. The tools are able to 'normalise' data into a common format, and then proceed with reconciling or pairing the positions. Once this process has been completed, the software performs a valuation comparison for each trade pair between the principal's and the counterparty's valuations. The results are then scanned, and any discrepancies in the form of unmatched trades are highlighted. The resulting information (trade pairs) is then ready to be sent to the disputing party together with a dispute notice that clearly displays details of unmatched transactions and mark-to-market valuations. The convenience that reconciliation modules offer in the form of storage of the historic reconciliation results and the translation details required to convert counterparty data into a common format also proves extremely useful and helps to facilitate future reconciliation processes.

Naturally, high trading volumes exacerbate the difficulties encountered in managing and resolving portfolio disputes, and since the determination of collateral requirements is based upon this data, it is crucial for users to be able to identify and reconcile differences in a timely manner.

Dependent upon source systems, file formats are not always identical, resulting in the need for 'normalisation' of data. For example, data fields may need to be jumbled, product groups created, and product reporting currency totals converted. Some flexibility is required to accommodate for errors, and allow users to search for and match trades according to parameter ranges. Most vanilla transactions can be matched relatively simply, but given that more institutions are moving into more exotic transactions, trade matching can prove more taxing. Structured transactions often create a mismatch of trades, as they may be booked in less sophisticated trading systems as multiple trades. For example, this can result in comparisons being made between a single trade and eight trades.

With such tight timeframes now stipulated in the documentation, most firms have little option but to move towards automating the entire reconciliation process. In addition, the ISDA Collateral Committee is currently working to produce a standardised file format for electronic data exchange during the portfolio reconciliation process. The working group's goal is to produce a reconciliation network, which utilises XML and ultimately FPML: messaging between counterparties.

Increasingly, this is incorporating the use of XML standards. Although many institutions have previously had to develop in-house solutions, the niche has been recognised by the market, and now a variety of vendor-provided solutions are being developed which will enable users to process portfolio reconciliations quickly and with minimum effort, and with no constraints in terms of trade volume.

CUSTODIAL INTERFACE

Once a margin requirement has been communicated and agreed by a client, instructions must be forwarded to the custody area to either receive or deliver the assets into an account. Collateral movement instructions can be communicated either verbally, by fax, or by e-mail to custodians, but increasingly collateral practitioners require systems to be built with custodial interfaces that allow for direct transmission of margin movement information. These interfaces support the provision of daily, intra-day or even real-time collateral position updates, automated or semi-automated instruction of incoming and outgoing collateral movements, and reconcile details of expected collateral holdings (collateral in transit) with actual custodial account records, providing users with an accurate overview of their collateral asset inventory.

These interfaces streamline the settlement processes, allowing users to register new assets, automatically generate custodial advice notices, and deliver a communication to the custody area instructing them of any pending movements. Information flows can be reversed, and custody systems relay information back to the collateral system, providing real-time updates of collateral positions, asset valuations, collateral in transit and notifying users of failed margin movements. Naturally, this reverse flow of information is critical in communicating to an institution whether a counterparty has not met their collateral obligation, which will need immediate escalation to the credit risk manager. However, it should be noted that it is of paramount importance that an application retains the flexibility to allow users to manually update collateral data in order to assess counterparty risk in the event of sudden market movements or in the absence of fed data.

MANAGEMENT REPORTING

Effective management reporting plays an important role in the process of properly managing collateralised exposures within an organisation. As a result, careful consideration must be given to the development of management reports. A collateral system should provide extensive management pre-defined and ad hoc reporting capabilities to support daily operational procedures and to assist in the prioritisation of tasks associated with the collateral management process. Additionally, extended reporting capabilities that allow for cross-agreement analysis of an entire client base are extremely useful from a credit management perspective, providing users with a risk management overview of the entire collateralised portfolio.

DATA ARCHIVING AND AUDIT

Data archiving and audit capabilities are key features of a solid, operational control environment. Therefore, it is essential for collateral technology to track the history of collateral movements, and be able to produce historical statement details. Although custodians are obliged to maintain detailed records for each collateral account, it is imperative for an institution to be able to tie-in asset deliveries with exposures associated with collateral agreements. A complete audit trail of deliveries and receipts will be required in the event of client default in addition to exposure summaries, and although custodial records can ultimately be referenced, client default situations tend to be hectic and time-critical. Therefore, it is far simpler and more time-efficient to be able to access accurate system records at any given moment directly using a collateral system which stores historic statements and reports, providing a complete and easily accessible, desktop-based collateral call history.

SECURITY AND USER ACCESS PERMISSIONS

Application security and user access level requirements also feature highly on the list of core functionality requirements, especially for larger organisations. Application security permits creation of multi-level group profiles and user privileges with the ability to assign multiple users to each profile, including read-only access. These profiles can be configured to represent internal infrastructure, business function and responsibilities as defined by the client. Security access rights should be granted at both group and individual levels, and able to cater for user-definable access levels to allow for 'read only' or 'read and write' access. The layers of these access levels should also be configurable at an even more granular level, at the demand of the system administrator or supervisor.

Collateral technology should, at a minimum, identify collateral which is available for rehypothecation within a collateralised portfolio. Many practitioners of rehypothecation rely upon spreadsheets in order to track asset location, and require their custodian to inform them of coupon payments and cash interest payments. However, more sophisticated technology may be purchased from vendors (or built in-house) that offers complete inventory management functionality. These solutions provide support for tracking asset re-use eligibility, internal policy on re-use, track asset location (details of collateral asset originators and recipients), calculation and distribution of coupons, cash management facilities, and manage the entire collateral management and asset allocation and inventory management process within one system.

DOWNSTREAM INFORMATION REPORTING REQUIREMENTS

Integrating collateral systems with credit risk systems, and incorporating collateral data into credit risk calculations is essential for effective corporate credit risk management. This is covered in greater detail in Chapter 10 'Incorporating collateral into credit exposure calculations'. When building a system, it is crucial to develop an architecture that supports downstream data feeds into a credit risk system for calculation of Value-at-Risk. Similarly, it is critical for an application to support user-friendly data extraction of new management information for risk management and reporting purposes in order to satisfy internal reporting requirements that may exceed current systems' existing reporting capabilities.

INVENTORY MANAGEMENT AND REHYPOTHECATION

In firms with large collateral management programmes, the collateral settlements team manage a large pool of collateral assets and requirements, and accordingly they need to optimise their asset portfolio in order to keep funding costs to a minimum. This can be achieved by re-using (otherwise referred to as rehypothecating) incoming collateral assets in order to satisfy their own outgoing collateral obligations. Rehypothecation rights granted within credit support documentation allow collateral managers to pool assets received under the agreement as credit support together with assets received as collateral under other credit support arrangements and re-use them, and is discussed in further detail in Chapter 9.

This pool of assets can be tapped into in order to fulfil collateral demands received from other collateralised counterparties, and a well co-ordinated inventory management effort presents a potentially powerful means of expanding firm liquidity and ultimately increasing revenues and minimising funding and operational costs. Identifying and selecting instruments from a pool of re-usable assets within a collateral portfolio can be a complex and time-consuming process to manage, but ultimately reduces, and in some cases eliminates, the cost of carry associated with financing collateral obligations. Increasingly, institutions are moving towards collateral asset management in order to maximise the potential of the asset pool which they control.

THE FUTURE OF COLLATERAL MANAGEMENT TECHNOLOGY

Traditionally, the collateralisation process has been managed on a specific, product-group basis, that is, for OTC Derivatives or repo. This is still the case in the vast majority of institutions, but it has been increasingly recognised as ineffective when estimating unsecured and secured counterparty exposure. Instead, the observed industry trend is that institutions are now leaning towards extended cross-product margining or enterprise collateral management in order to achieve a complete view of credit risk. This is now promoted as best practice by the ISDA Collateral Committee.

As a preliminary step in the right direction, many institutions are choosing to centralise their margin departments, but are still relying on several different systems in order to achieve a firm-wide view of credit risk. When considering exposure to a particular party, it is prudent to measure the 'whole counterparty' exposure since upon default the entire portfolio will be affected, not just the particular product silo. Single-product collateralisation does not allow for netting of exposures in the event of default, and may actually lead to increased loss within a portfolio since mark-to-market gains may not be netted with mark-to-market losses. On this note, as indicated in the ISDA Margin Survey 2001, all respondents support OTC Derivatives, but in addition, repo, structured products, SPVs and FX margin trading were supported by well over one third of respondents. A considerable proportion (between 19% and 30%) of organizations also reported providing collateral management for other product types, such as loans, exchange traded derivative products, and securities lending.

Naturally, the increasing trend towards centralised margining also places extra demands on the capabilities of collateral technology and staff. The need to streamline data and information flows across various segmented business lines, and integrate single-product margin requirements into a collateralised portfolio environment, is of paramount importance in order to manage data in a controlled manner. One immediate success of adopting this approach is the clarity of an institution's collateral position and associated exposure. This should prove advantageous in times of market crisis, when any margin department requires absolute transparency in reporting its positions, and assessing and controlling exposure.

The other major stress on collateral management systems comes from expanding volumes of collateral agreements. An increasing number of firms manage more than 2000 OTC Derivatives collateral agreements across multiple locations, resulting in a need for collateral management systems to support volume as well as complexity.

CHAPTER 9

THE IMPACT OF COLLATERAL ON CORPORATE LIQUIDITY

As we have seen, a collateral management programme, even if it is very well run, has far-reaching impacts on the rest of a firm. This is particularly true in the case of collateral and corporate liquidity.

DEFINING ELIGIBLE COLLATERAL

A firm's definition of eligible collateral is crucial when thinking about the impacts on corporate liquidity. Although each firm will draw up its own list, within the collateral policy, generic good-quality collateral does have some consistent characteristics:

- An asset over which it is easy to perfect a security interest
- Highly liquid
- Of good credit quality
- Easy to value
- Easy to settle.

Collateral assets having such qualities should be easier than others to sell for a fair market value in the event of the counterparty's default, even in times of market stress. An additional benefit of high-quality collateral, however, is that it is that much more attractive for the purposes of collateral re-use.

THE IMPACT OF COLLATERAL
ON CORPORATE LIQUIDITY

COLLATERAL ASSETS USED TO SECURE DERIVATIVES EXPOSURE

The ISDA Margin Survey 2001[11] reported that the most common assets employed as collateral are US government securities and cash. This has not changed over recent years. The survey reported that cash is used more frequently as collateral by institutions and this is gaining in popularity for two reasons. The first is that the available pool of US government securities is reducing, and the second is the operational convenience that cash offers. According to ISDA, over 90% of collateral programmes accept, and hold, cash and US government securities as collateral. Euro and Sterling denominated cash and securities are close behind, with 65%–70% of firms holding collateral in this form. Japanese Yen denominated assets (typically Japanese Government Bonds and yen cash) are held by just under 60% of respondents. The survey reported just 20%–25% of participants using equities and corporate bonds as collateral. As expected, such assets tend to be of the highest grade. Typically, the equities used are members of major indices (such as S&P 500) and corporate bonds tend to be AAA rated.

Interestingly, according to ISDA, over 70% of institutions report that they actively re-use (or rehypothecate) incoming collateral assets in order to satisfy their own outgoing collateral obligations. This process can be extremely labour-intensive, but ultimately reduces, and in some cases eliminates, the cost of carry associated with financing collateral requirements outside of the collateral management programme. Taking this process one step further, between 55% and 65% also report the active repo of collateral assets, and re-use of collateral to support their firm's liquidity requirements. By actively investing and trading the assets within a collateral book, institutions are able to partially finance their collateral operations, and reduce the financial burden to the firms of what is otherwise typically a cost centre.

SOURCES OF COLLATERAL

When a firm has a collateral programme in place, arrangements need to be in place to source the collateral requirements which arise. Generally, an institution will turn to its repo and/or liquidity desk to provide the assets to meet these collateral requirements. The margin department must repo in securities or, alternatively, borrow cash in sufficient quantities to cover the unsecured, out-of-the-money exposures. The desks go out into the market to determine the cheapest-to-deliver assets in order to minimise the cost-of-carry associated with financing collateral obligations. When an institution is making frequent collateral calls, it is not unusual to retain a conservative amount of assets in a general pool to cover collateral delivery demands that result from increasing out-of-the-money exposures. In the event that such a pool is maintained, these proprietary assets may be used to pledge out as credit support. In addition, incoming assets that have been delivered by counterparties to cover in-the-money exposures and whose documentation specifies rehypothecation eligibility, may be re-used to satisfy an institution's outgoing collateral obligations, and further reduce operating costs.

In situations where an institution does not have readily available access to borrowing assets internally (for example small hedge funds), they may wish to purchase the assets from the very same counterparty that requires the delivery of credit support. In this instance, the pledgor executes a standard purchase of securities from the secured party's finance desk, and may elect to settle the transaction in one of two ways. They may either send (or wire) the cash payment directly into the repo desk's settlement account, who then become responsible for transferring the securities internally into the purchasing party's collateral account, or deliver the cash payment directly into their collateral account. From here the collateral settlements team must execute an internal transfer of cash to the repo desk's settlement account. As soon as the cash hits the second account, the securities are simultaneously transferred to the named collateral account. This exchange of assets for cash is referred to as a 'Delivery versus Payment' (DVP) or 'Receipt versus Payment' (RVP), depending on whether the assets are being delivered or received into your account in exchange for cash.

Given the increasing number of collateral assets in circulation, the typical collateral operations team must work very closely with the trading desks that source the instruments. Cash collateral, for example, needs to be carefully managed in order to reap a satisfactory rate of return. Reinvestment of cash collateral yields returns that must be used to satisfy cash interest payments due to the pledgor under the terms of the credit support documentation. Surplus capitalised interest payments arising from the reinvestment may then be retained by the desk to offset any fees owed by the collateral operations department in return for their collateral sourcing and reinvestment services.

Typically, the collateral settlement team provides the liquidity desk with daily cash predictions in order to maximise the return on their cash collateral. These predictions would ordinarily consist of a daily report that provides a complete itemisation of the incoming and outgoing cash collateral payments for that day. Any incoming cash payments may be reinvested back into the market, while the report serves to notify the desk how much cash must be put aside to deliver out to collateralised counterparties. As you may imagine, this report needs to be prepared as early as possible in the working day, and sent out to the desk so that they may factor the requirements into their daily business transactions.

Similarly, the collateral settlements team must also work with the repo or finance desk on a daily basis to ensure that any securities pledged out by the party may be considered to be the 'cheapest-to-deliver' option at all times. Daily reports must be prepared noting all incoming and outgoing deliveries of securities, and daily reconciliations between the repo desk's inventory record and the collateral team's system must be made in order to keep track of their positions, enabling rapid recall or substitution of securities as and when required.

Although manually intensive, the reasons behind the 'cheapest-to-deliver' driver are valid. For example, Bank A may need to fund a short position with a particular issue of securities, and may be willing to pay over the odds to borrow or buy the instrument at short notice. If Bank B is able to locate that particular issue within the pool of collateral on loan to the collateral department, they would ordinarily request that it be returned and swapped or substituted for cheaper, alternative (but eligible) securities. This would then enable Bank B to sell or loan the securities to Bank A, and command a good price with a profitable spread. This requires smart operational process to organise daily substitutions of assets that may either be held as part of a pool of collateral or may be pledged out to counterparties as credit support, in order to free up and mobilise more lucrative assets for repo and stock borrowing and loan purposes.

CENTRALISED COLLATERAL ASSET AND LIABILITY MANAGEMENT

As collateralisation in the marketplace expands, the collateral settlements team manage an increasing pool of collateral assets, and need to optimise their asset portfolio in order to keep funding costs to a minimum. This can be achieved by re-using incoming collateral assets in order to satisfy their own outgoing collateral obligations. Rehypothecation permissions granted within credit support documentation allow collateral managers to pool assets received under the agreement as credit support, together with assets received as collateral under other credit support arrangements, and use them for alternative purposes.

The pool of assets can then be tapped into in order to fulfil collateral demands received from other collateralised counterparties, and a well co-ordinated inventory management effort presents a potentially powerful means of expanding firm liquidity and ultimately increasing revenues and minimising funding and operational costs. Identifying and selecting instruments from a pool of re-usable assets within a collateral portfolio can be a complex and time-consuming process to manage, but ultimately reduces and in some cases eliminates the cost of carry associated with financing collateral obligations. Increasingly, institutions are moving towards collateral asset management in order to maximise the potential of the asset pool which they control. By actively investing the assets within a collateral book, the collateral management team take on the dual role of the margin managers and to a certain degree the role of the repo traders.

It is standard market practice to adopt a corporate policy which states that all collateral assets be managed by the financing business units in order to ensure optimal re-use. Ideally, all assets received under a title transfer agreement or a pledge agreement with the appropriate re-use permissions should be included in the inventory. Any asset held under a pledge agreement that does not specify re-use eligibility rights must be held in a segregated collateral account by the secured party's custodian for safe-keeping.

FUNDING A COLLATERAL MANAGEMENT PROGRAMME

When negotiating collateral agreements, it is extremely important to consider the impact of any interest rates agreed between the two parties for cash collateral. Although it's important to negotiate a fair rate of return on pledged cash, it's even more important to be able to lock into an agreed rate that is pragmatic for an institution, in order to maintain a stable and hopefully profitable spread. So, in the event that the counterparty decides to deliver cash collateral, interest earnings above and beyond a contractual rate may be used to offset or minimise (the latter of which is more likely) any expenses associated with the process. These expenses may include transaction costs relating to the investment of the funds by a corporate liquidity desk and the costs of opening and maintaining a custodial cash account. Theoretically, it is in every institution's best interests to negotiate interest payment terms that will contribute to or, more desirably, eliminate the cost of carry. Practically speaking, it is not always possible to recuperate the cost of carry in the amounts of interest received and paid, so although many companies have strong aspirations to establish the function as a profit centre, as opposed to a cost centre, this is not always achievable in practice.

In order to defray the costs of a collateral management function, the unit needs to charge back the cost of providing the service to the business it supports. Methods include charging desks for the number of deals that are collateralised, the number of agreements supported and the level of manual intervention required according to the complexity of the transaction valuation methods, all of which are then translated into a cost equivalent.

Cost centre allocation rules determine the costs of funding, net of rehypothecation, and also calculate any benefits arising from collateralisation that are to be applied to each business unit. These benefits are realised in the form of increased trading lines, more competitive pricing due to a reduced credit charge, and possibly a share of returns from rehypothecated assets. Business units receive these credits for the implementation of collateral agreements, and ordinarily the business unit that sponsored the negotiation and implementation of the collateral agreement reaps the benefits of these credits.

Credits may also be received in the form of credit charge rebates that are awarded in institutions where credit charges exist. Some market participants are sophisticated enough to be able to factor in the cost of credit into their derivatives pricing models. These pricing models then effectively transfer some or all of the cost of credit onto their client. These charges are often paid upon the execution of a transaction in order to secure a credit risk manager's approval and may be thought of as a form of credit insurance. The payment of this charge results in any loss arising from the transaction being absorbed by the company, and not by the individual business unit. Usually, the size of the credit charge reflects the future potential credit loss, and accordingly such charges are reduced in the event that a collateral agreement is signed. Businesses usually pay the fee upfront, and once the benefit of collateralisation has been factored in, the charge is rebated.

If a collateral management unit is to be run as a profit centre, allocation rules need to incorporate both funding and expenses. Funding costs are directed back to the individual business units, and a profit-generating service charge is added. This service charge would usually cover the cost of implementing and maintaining collateral technology and operational resources, custodial account operating and maintenance fees, and a general handling charge for the service provided by the collateral management team.

MEASURING AND MANAGING COLLATERAL LIQUIDITY RISK

In the event of a credit rating downgrade, a party must be prepared to respond to increased collateral demands from its counterparties if thresholds are tied to counterparty credit ratings. The institution must be able to meet those delivery requirements within the designated time period, as stipulated by the credit support documentation, in order to avoid an event of default. The need to meet those demands could place incredible strain upon a corporation's liquidity, given that the institution would have to free-up considerable amounts of assets at a moment's notice in order to meet those demands, particularly at the time when funding costs will have increased.

The Bank of England's 1982 policy notice on 'the measurement of liquidity' set out four key principles of prudent liquidity management. It stated that:

> A bank should be able to meet its obligations as and when they fall due. It should maintain sufficient, immediately available cash or liquid assets to meet its

obligations. It should have an appropriately matched future profile of cashflows from maturing assets; and it should have an adequately diversified deposit base in terms of both maturities and range of counterparties.

Participants in the collateralised market need to measure the worst-case scenarios in terms of liquidity risk. By way of precaution, most institutions have in place some form of risk management that allows senior management to assess the impact of worst-case scenarios, such as unexpected downgrades. This is likely to be in the form of daily operating reports that the collateral department can create and distribute to their management team and finance desks for consultation. The reports allow them to qualify who their credit rating contingent counterparties are, and quantify the incremental collateral demands that they would have to meet based upon current mark-to-market exposure, in the event of a downgrade.

At the most basic level, the typical format of a liquidity stress-testing model should report upon changes in party and counterparty credit ratings, and provide summary information as to how these changes would affect the amount of incoming and outgoing collateral requirements. Subsequently, the report should quantify the potential demands placed upon the liquidity and finance desks to source these obligations in the event of a party downgrade.

One might also report on the effect of counterparty ratings changes. These reports offer some value by allowing users to calculate how much collateral would be freed up and returned to the trading desks in the event of a counter-party downgrade, or how much incremental collateral would be required in the event of an upgrade. Credit managers may suspect an imminent downgrade or upgrade of a counterparty or a group of counterparties, and these reports help them to understand and communicate the impact of ratings changes to the appropriate funding desks and business managers. The report content for a standard 'ratings-watch' report should include credit-rating contingent para-meters (scale of thresholds, minimum transfer amounts and rounding amounts at each rating level), current credit ratings and applicable threshold, minimum transfer and rounding amount data. It should also display the current mark-to-market value for each credit rating contingent relationship, current levels of collateral pledged by the principal party and incremental amounts of collateral that the principal party would need to deliver in the event of a single down-grade (that is, by one rating level). The incremental collateral requirement should be expressed both as a monetary value and a percentage, and the report should also give the user the option to view the incremental requirements if the downgrade was by more than one rating level.

More sophisticated liquidity stress-testing models may be incorporated into credit risk exposure engines, which allow users to manipulate data further and run market scenarios. These simulations enable credit management teams and finance desks to predict the impact of collateral upon corporate liquidity in the event of interest rates changes or dramatic movements in currency exchange rates. These scenarios may be loosely based upon the current market conditions and trends, or may be entirely speculative for producing worst-case scenarios. Ideally, these models allow users to tweak a variety of data and to be able to create a variety of situations, either in isolation or in combination. For example, the ability to adjust both individual currency pairs (that is, GBP/USD rate drops by 5%), or specify a general rise of a particular currency (that is, GBP drop by 2% against any combination of currencies). Similarly, users need to be able to identify how a rise in interest rates, no matter how small, would impact the net exposure of a collateral portfolio and, in contrast, what effect an adverse change in rates may have upon the same portfolio. Additional, particularly useful data manipulation patterns may include tweaking the value of individual instruments, or groups of asset types to further enhance the value of any collateralised portfolio stress test. This type of reporting proves extremely useful for credit managers. For example, a user may want to estimate the impact of devaluation of the Argentinean Peso upon agreements that are secured by the currency, or measure how a sharp decrease in the valuation of Mexican Brady Bonds would affect their portfolios secured by these assets. Similarly, the ability to measure how changes in issuer ratings affect collateral valuation percentages (or haircuts) is of immense use by allowing users to calculate the potential incremental collateral requirements arising from the application of more conservative haircuts to the asset valuations. Asset managers may then be consulted to determine whether there is any worth in reinvesting these otherwise illiquid assets in order to maximise the return on the already interest-bearing assets for risk reduction purposes.

Combinations of scenarios provide users with the most realistic look at how their collateralised portfolio may be affected – an economic crisis in one specific geographic location can often spark a chain of events that result in a chain of market downturns across all sectors of the financial industry. An example of this would be that a number of UK banks are downgraded, UK bond prices fall, sterling is weakened and the GBP/USD rate drops sharply.

The ability to run these simulations provides credit managers with the capability to determine at a glance how much incremental collateral would be required in the event of a market crisis. These reporting capabilities also provide senior management with an excellent sense of the potential scope of such a scenario upon the company's resources, allowing them to define and implement controls and procedures in order to minimise the impact of such events upon the corporation's assets.

PART III

The Effects
of Taking
Collateral

CHAPTER 10

INCORPORATING COLLATERAL INTO CREDIT EXPOSURE CALCULATIONS

INTRODUCTION

There are three main techniques for mitigating credit risk. A credit officer can enhance a counterparty's credit by pursuing actions that reduce the company's net exposure to that counterparty in the event that the counterparty defaults (for example by signing master agreements to facilitate the netting of deal exposures), reduce the probability of the counterparty defaulting on its obligations (for example by obtaining a guarantee on the counterparty from another company) and increase the recovery rate in the event that the counterparty defaults (for example by negotiating senior creditor status for the company).

Netting can be a very powerful tool for reducing the credit exposure, especially for counterparties with large proportions of derivative transactions in their portfolios. US financial institutions active in the derivatives market use netting to reduce their gross exposure to counterparties by more than 60 per cent. In general, the larger the number of deals outstanding with a given counterparty, the larger the proportion of derivatives transactions in the counterparty's portfolio, the closer the maturities and the more evenly balanced the portfolio between receiving and paying in each currency, then the larger the reduction in credit exposure to that counterparty created by netting. But netting is only effective if there are negative mark-to-market deal values to offset positive exposures (for example, netting cannot reduce counterparty credit exposure when there are only loans outstanding to the counterparty) and can only mitigate, not manage, counterparty credit exposure. The most effective tool for actively managing counterparty credit exposure is collateral management.

The purpose of this chapter is to set out how collateral reduces both current and potential exposure, and how collateral can be managed to minimise credit exposure. But before discussing collateral management, we need to discuss the alternative techniques currently used for measuring counterparty credit exposure.

THE NOTIONAL LOAN APPROACH TO MODELLING CREDIT EXPOSURE

Since accounting for loans is based on notional, rather than mark-to-market, value, and bankruptcy courts generally rely on loans' notional values to quantify creditors' claims, it is natural to set the potential credit exposure of a loan equal to the notional loan amount outstanding, plus accrued interest, at that given time. The potential credit exposure profile over the life of a loan is normally quite stable, independent of both market and credit conditions, and is always significantly positive. Another loan or line of credit to the same counterparty can only add to the exposure. Although this approach can be misleading for long-term low coupon debt instruments (whose earlier mark-to-market values can be significantly less than the final promised repayment), using the sum of the projected loan balances to estimate a counterparty's potential credit exposure profile is both simple and relatively accurate for floating rate debt and short-term fixed rate debt instruments.

But the notional loan amount approach is inappropriate for the many financial instruments whose values are linked poorly, if at all, to their notional values and are quite unstable over time since they are dependent on either market or credit conditions, and may be negative as well as positive. The very diverse range of potential credit exposure profiles for various instruments is illustrated in Table 10.1.

The examples in Table 10.1 should also make it clear that concentrating on current exposure, although acceptable for loans, is entirely inappropriate for other financial instruments. Many financial instruments, such as out-of-the-money options, that have small current exposures could have very large exposures if favourable scenarios occur.

Making a further loan to a counterparty can only increase potential exposure. But the fact that some financial instruments can have negative mark-to-market values means that the appropriate choice of an additional deal may reduce, rather than increase, a counterparty's credit exposure. For example,

Table 10.1 Credit exposure profiles

Instrument	Expected exposure	Distribution of exposure
Floating rate loan	Constant over time	Independent of interest rates
Zero coupon bond	Grows exponentially	Increases if interest rates fall
Interest rate swap (paying fixed rate)	Increase at first, then decrease towards zero	Increases if interest rates rise
Cross-currency swap (paying strong currency)	Becomes increasingly negative over time	Increases if weak currency strengthens
Commodity swap (paying fixed rate)	Approximately zero	Increases if commodity price increases

purchasing a credit default swap will reduce the potential credit exposure profile for a counterparty with an outstanding loan.

It has therefore become standard practice to use notional exposures to measure current and potential exposure for loans and bonds, and to use mark-to-market and mark-to-model values to measure current and potential exposure for other financial instruments.

THE MARK-TO-MODEL APPROACH TO MODELLING CREDIT EXPOSURE

One approach to measuring potential credit exposure incorporates the Bank for International Settlements (BIS) model, which calculates the capital required to be held by OECD banks against their derivative portfolios. Credit exposure in this model is the sum of the deal's current mark-to-market value and a potential exposure add-on, ranging from 0% to 15% of the deal's notional principal outstanding, depending on the type of deal and its remaining maturity. Unfortunately, this model's simplicity is more than offset by its inaccuracy. For example, the expected credit exposure for the cross-currency swap in Table 10.1 depends critically on which currency is expected to strengthen over the life of the deal. Yet the BIS model assigns exactly the same add-on, regardless of whether the counterparty is paying the strengthening currency or the weakening currency. Given this inability of the current BIS model to reflect the nuances of all but the simplest of financial instruments, the Basel Committee's June 1999 'Internal Ratings-based Approach' consultative paper sets out a new method for calculating credit exposure. The committee now proposes that the level of 'Exposure at the time of default' will be the relevant measure of credit exposure. Given that default can occur at any time in the future, we must therefore model both current exposure and potential exposure at every relevant future point until the maturity of the longest deal with a given counterparty.

The general approach to modelling potential credit exposure is very similar to that used to measure Value-at-Risk (VAR) using Monte Carlo simulations: identify the market and credit risk factors affecting the value of the financial instruments, model the joint distribution of these variables, use this joint distribution to simulate values of these variables and then map from these simulated risk factor values to a distribution of values of the financial instruments. Because a counterparty's credit exposure profile is a function of the potential mark-to-market values of the deals currently outstanding with that counterparty, it depends partly on exactly the same variables that impact the market risk of a derivatives portfolio (interest rate, equity and commodity yield and volatility curves, and foreign exchange rates) and partly on the correlations between these variables.

SCENARIO ANALYSIS

If there are only a few relevant risk variables, negligible correlations and the value of the deals is computed from the underlying risk variables using simple, monotonic formulae, scenario analysis is sufficient to model the potential exposure profile. Take, for example, a portfolio of swaps, caps and floors executed in one currency. The 2 standard deviation 'stressed case' potential credit exposure at any future time, t, can be modelled by first valuing the deals in the counterparty's portfolio with an 'upward shift' forward interest rate curve in which each expected forward rate from time t onwards is increased by two or three times the volatility appropriate for the maturity. If netting is appropriate, the deals' values at time t are summed to create the portfolio's value at time t under this scenario. If netting is inappropriate, then negative deal values are first set to zero, and the deals' values are then summed.

The process is then repeated with a similarly constructed 'downward shift' curve. The higher of these two portfolio values is taken as the potential exposure of the portfolio at time t. Repeating this procedure for the remaining life of the portfolio of financial instruments creates the potential exposure profile for a counterparty, and also identifies the scenario to which the portfolio is most vulnerable at each point in the future. This scenario approach should not be confused with the 'worst-case' approach to measuring potential credit exposure. For example, if the expected exposure at time t for a portfolio of interest rate swaps is 252,000 Euros, the 2 sigma upward shift exposure is 267,000 Euros and the 2 sigma downward shift exposure is 236,000 Euros, then the portfolio's potential exposure at time t is 267,000 Euros, and the portfolio is vulnerable to a rise in interest rates at time t. However, if we added the 'worst-case' values for each deal, we would create an exposure of 317,000 Euros at time t – an overestimate because the approach adds deal values created when interest rates rise to deal values created when interest rates fall.

But there are several problems with this 'shift' approach, and it does not guarantee accuracy. For example, the stressed case exposure for financial instruments that do not have a monotonic link between risk variables and deal values, such as range forward notes, will not occur on either the upward or downward interest rate shift parts, but on some interior interest rate path. If the counterparty's portfolio includes a number of interest rate swaps and the counterparty is predominantly receiving fixed at short maturities and paying fixed at longer maturities, then a 2 sigma twist, rather than shift, of the yield curve would be needed in order to identify the 'stressed case' potential exposure profile. But the biggest problem occurs when the number of risk variables increases. Even if you assume independence between these variables, n variables require 2^n scenarios, and that can be computationally burdensome; and the assumption of independence between risk factors is becoming more suspect in an increasingly inter-linked global economy. But scenario analysis should not be ignored – it has some strong points. The regular analysis of both historical scenarios ('what would the counterparty's exposure be if the 1998 Asian crisis repeated itself?') and possible scenarios ('what if a majority in the next Quebec referendum votes "oui"?') can be of considerable value to credit officers concerned about potential counterparty exposures.

MONTE CARLO SIMULATION

As the number of relevant risk variables increases, the importance of modelling the correlation between these variables increases, and the simplified approaches discussed above give way to the Monte Carlo simulation approach to estimating potential credit exposure.

The first step in this simulation process is to determine the relevant risk factors – interest rates, commodity prices, equity indices, FX rates, and so on – that impact the value of the deals in a counterparty's portfolio. Given that Monte Carlo simulation is inherently time-consuming, and highly accurate deal valuations are not required, it is common practise to minimise the number of risk factors used. For example, a maximum of three interest rate risk factors, rather than the dozen or more generally used in market VAR simulations, can be used to describe each currency's yield curve. The second step is to model the joint evolution of these risk factors. To reduce computation time, it is usual to assume that the risk factors follow a Brownian motion process with constant drift and volatility parameters, requiring the estimation of a variance/covariance matrix for these factors. The third step is to simulate the evolution of these risk factors from today until the final maturity of the counterparty's deals. The fourth step is to choose intermediate times for valuing the counterparty's deals. The simplest approach is to choose arbitrary time intervals, which may range from monthly for the first year to annually in ten years' time. A more sophisticated approach would choose the dates on which large cash flows could occur. However, if a portfolio includes options, such as swaptions, which can be exercised into other transactions, rather than cash, the time periods chosen must be sufficiently dense to allow for exercise of these options at the appropriate times. On each of these dates, the simulated values of the underlying risk factors are used to value each deal. This process is repeated for each set of simulated values, creating a distribution of values for each deal on that date.

Once the deal values have been simulated on a given date, the next step is to combine these deal values to create the counterparty's potential credit exposure. First, combine the values of all deals that can be netted. Then set any negative values for this 'super' deal and the non-nettable deals with this counterparty to zero, and sum the positive values. (Suppressing these negative values entirely is not recommended, since credit officers can profitably assign these deals to financial intermediaries with positive exposures to that counterparty.) Repeating this calculation for each set of simulated values creates a distribution of potential credit exposures for the counterparty on that date.

It is customary to graph the average and stressed case (ex. 95%) exposures for a counterparty, as illustrated in Figure 10.1. In this example, FX transactions dominate the first year and the average exposure drops thereafter. In year 5, and again in years 8 and 9, we expect to owe the counterparty money, but both the average and stressed case exposures rise thereafter, reflecting the fact that we are receiving the strengthening currency in a long-dated cross-currency swap.

The Monte Carlo simulation approach also facilitates a more detailed analysis of the 5% of the simulations that create the largest exposures at any future time. The deals that contribute most to the largest exposures at each future point in time can be identified (in the above example, the major contributor to large simulated exposures in later years is the cross-currency swap), as can the factor movements that underlie these exposures. A credit officer can therefore use Monte Carlo simulations to manage, as well as measure and monitor counterparty credit risk. In the above example, the counterparty could be offered relatively advantageous terms for any longer-dated cross-currency deals in which the counterparty received a strengthening currency, since these deals would be negatively correlated with the outstanding cross-currency swap.

Before discussing how to incorporate collateral into Monte Carlo simulations of credit exposure, we need to revisit the choice of relevant risk factors.

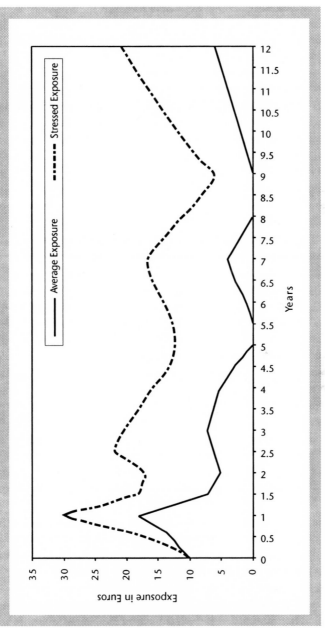

Figure 10.1 Counterparty credit exposure

One approach, used in several credit simulation models, is to follow the convention used in market VAR calculations and consider only market factors, implicitly assuming that deal values are independent of changes in default probabilities. For many instruments, such as FX contracts and interest rate swaps, this is a reasonable assumption. But for other instruments, for example a single name credit default swap whose most important risk factor is the reference credit's probability of default, it is not reasonable to assume that default probabilities remain constant for the multi-year time periods considered in credit simulations. A diametrically opposite approach, taken by CreditMetrics, is to set market risk factors at their expected levels on future dates and calculate loan or bond values as a function of the counterparty's simulated default probability. For a standard bank-provided line of credit, the draw-down, and therefore the potential exposure, can be critically affected by the counterparty's default probability (Xerox increased the utilisation of its credit lines significantly in 2001 when rating downgrades forced it out of the Commercial Paper market).

When including default probabilities as relevant risk factors for measuring potential credit exposure, one approach is to assume that they are independent of the other relevant risk factors, which simplifies the computational burden. But this assumption ignores the empirical evidence that links default rates to macro-economic variables. More reasonably, KMV and CreditMetrics model the correlations between default probabilities, implicitly assuming that there are no credit cycles. CreditPortfolioView goes further, explicitly modelling the time series behaviour of default rates – linking it to market risk factors such as interest rates and FX rates – and saves computational time by assuming that correlations between default probabilities can be entirely explained by changes in these macro-economic variables. Specifically, CreditPortfolioView first simulates a 'state of nature' – a certain set of macro-economic variables – and then estimates default probabilities conditional on this state of nature. These conditional default probability estimates are considered independent. (If these conditional default probabilities differ across states of nature, then the marginal default probabilities can exhibit correlations similar to those used in the KMV and CreditMetrics models.)

A simple example may illustrate the importance of modelling changes in default rates if default rates affect potential credit exposure. Standard & Poor's has published ratings transition matrices for each of the past 20+ years. Each of these transition matrices can be linked to the levels and changes in the levels of macro-economic variables such as GNP, unemployment, equity indices, interest rates and FX rates that year. Now assume that we are simulating the evolution of the current levels of these risk factors over time. Then, given the values of these variables for each intermediate future point in time, we can choose an appropriate ratings transition matrix. Since the downgrade and default probabilities shown in these transition matrices for a company with a given initial rating vary by a factor of 2 to 3, the probability of simulating a downgrade or default in that period varies significantly. The choice of the appropriate transition matrix can therefore have a significant impact on the potential exposure of credit lines and credit default swaps.

INCORPORATING COLLATERAL

For the purposes of this discussion, we assume that the collateral management function is being performed effectively – that each item of collateral is properly documented, operationally controlled, legally perfected (if necessary) and that legal research has assigned a probability that our claim on that collateral will be legally enforceable in insolvency.

In general, positive collateral balances can offset current exposures, and positive collateral balances held in the future may offset potential credit exposure. But it is much simpler to measure the ability of currently held collateral to offset positive exposures than it is to measure the impact of collateral on future potential exposures. There may be uncertainties as to the mark-to-market value and the legal enforceability of collateral currently held, but at least we know what collateral is being held. In the previous section, we showed how the simulated values of the underlying risk factors are used to value the deals outstanding with the counterparty at each relevant future point in time. But in order to simulate the value of collateral at a future point in time, we need to know what collateral would have held at that time. The answer to this question is determined by calculating what collateral would have been required, under the terms of the collateral agreement, at the previous remarking. We therefore need first to model the terms of the collateral agreement with that counterparty.

TERMS OF THE COLLATERAL AGREEMENT

The concepts underlying counterparty collateral management, with marking-to-market of positions on a regular basis, together with the related posting and return of collateral, are the same as the concepts underlying futures exchange margining systems, with several small differences. Exchanges require that initial and variation margin be posted, that positions be remarked daily, that margin be posted in cash or short maturity government securities and that margin requirements be met exactly. However, counterparties may agree to only post margin above a threshold (which can itself be set as a function of a counterparty's credit ratings), can agree to a longer period, such as a month or a quarter, between remarkings (the trade-off is that, although the operational costs are reduced by lengthening the remarking period, the probability of the collateral being inadequate is increased), may agree to post collateral in a wide range of domestic and foreign securities and assets (with different 'haircuts' – valuation percentages – for each class and/or maturity of assets) and agree to minimum transfer and rounding amounts.

Once we have modelled these elements of the counterparty collateral system, there are several other points that have to be addressed before we can measure the impact of collateral agreements on potential credit exposure. Assume first that we are measuring the impact of collateral on the current exposure of a counterparty. The physical collateral currently posted was determined at the last collateral remarking date. The calculations made at that date first used the details of the collateral agreement, including threshold amounts, minimum transfer amounts and so on, to determine the 'cash equivalent' collateral to be held, and then checked that the net value of the eligible physical collateral posted, after the relevant haircuts had been applied, matched this amount.

If the counterparty defaults today, time will elapse (for contractual, market liquidity or statutory reasons) before the transactions with that counterparty can be terminated and the collateral liquidated. During this period, generally known as the 'cure' period, the value of both the deals and the collateral, and therefore the final net exposure, will be subject to change because of market moves. So, in order to estimate the potential exposure, net of collateral posted, at a given date in the future, we first have to subtract the remarking period from that date to determine the prior remarking date. We then simulate the relevant market risk parameters up to the prior remarking date and, based on the simulated deal values, determine how much collateral will be posted as of that date. Next, we simulate the behaviour of these market factors in the period between the prior remarking date and the end of the cure period, calculate the value of both the deals and the collateral instruments at the end of the cure period, and then determine the net exposure to that counterparty at that future point in time.

RATINGS-BASED THRESHOLDS

Three further complications can then arise. The first complication is that if the collateral agreement specifies thresholds that are dependent on ratings, we also have to simulate the paths of both parties' ratings from today until the given prior remarking date. To accomplish this, the rating transition matrices provided by the major rating agencies can be used. It has been customary to use their average annual transition matrices for this purpose, but, as pointed out above, the transition probabilities for a given year can vary from these average transition probabilities quite significantly. If the thresholds change considerably with rating changes, it would be better not to use the average transition matrix, but to choose that set of annual transition matrices which best fits the simulated path of a simple set of macro-economic variables such as ΔGNP, Δunemployment rates and Δshort term interest rates.

ELIGIBLE COLLATERAL

The second complication occurs if the list of eligible collateral includes a wide range of instruments in several currencies. In order to simulate the changes in value of the posted collateral between the prior remarking date and the end of the cure period (which may extend a week, a fortnight or more, depending on the legal environment, beyond the simulation date), we have to know what collateral was posted on the prior remarking date.

The simplest way of handling this problem is to stop the collateral selection process after determining the 'cash equivalent' amount, and assume that the collateral posted on the prior remarking date has this same cash equivalent value at the end of the cure period. But this approach has the potential drawback that if the collateral posted was long-dated Treasury bonds, the simulated market factor changes may be sufficiently severe (a significant increase in long-term interest rates) to reduce the simulated market values of the collateral below the cash equivalent amount. In this circumstance, the cash equivalent approach would underestimate the potential credit exposure at the end of the cure period.

We can address this problem by assuming that all collateral is posted in one instrument and, after determining the amount of this collateral posted on the prior remarking date, simulate the value of this instrument at the end of the cure period. At present, many collateral agreements between dealer banks restrict the eligible collateral to a relatively small number of US Treasuries, and therefore this approach is entirely appropriate. But collateral agreements with corporations often include a much wider range of eligible collateral – commodity inventories, physical equipment such as aircraft, railway rolling stock (because of the standard track gauge throughout the US, standard railroad car wagons have been widely accepted as collateral for over a century) and ships, royalty rights, and financial claims in other currencies. Although it can be significantly more difficult to model the behaviour of these assets, it may be necessary to do so in order to estimate potential exposure more accurately, and it does provide a significant side benefit – it allows a credit officer to model the impact of correlations between the value of the deals outstanding with a counterparty and the collateral posted, and therefore provides guidance as to which collateral is most desirable in given scenarios.

THE ENFORCEABILITY OF COLLATERAL PROVISIONS

The third complication is the fact that, although a collateral agreement may be in place with a counterparty, there may be some doubt as to whether or not the agreement will be legally enforceable. This complication can be addressed by including a 'Collateral Confidence Factor' – the probability that a collateral agreement with counterparty X in jurisdiction Y will be enforceable as written during insolvency – in the simulation. This probability can be easily modelled as an independent binomial distribution, but estimating this probability for a given jurisdiction may require serious legal research.

USING THE CORRELATION BETWEEN DEAL AND ASSET VALUES TO IDENTIFY DESIRABLE COLLATERAL

For counterparties with collateral agreements, the principal determinants of variations in net potential credit exposure around the agreed threshold levels are the movements in the relevant underlying risk factors in the time between the prior remarking and the end of the cure period, and the correlations between the value of the outstanding deals and the posted collateral. If the eligible collateral is restricted to cash or US bills and notes, the value of the collateral will be independent of market moves and therefore uncorrelated with deal values. The change in credit exposure between the prior remarking and the end of the cure period will then be entirely a function of changes in deal values caused by changes in the underlying risk factors. However, if the eligible collateral included a longer-dated US bond, its value would be highly positively correlated with the values of any longer-dated, receiving fixed-interest rate US dollar interest rate swaps outstanding. Because of this positive correlation, such a bond would significantly reduce the impact of interest rate decreases on potential credit exposure. Conversely, if the deal portfolio included longer-dated, paying fixed-interest rate US dollar interest rate swaps, this bond would increase, rather than decrease, the impact of an interest rate decrease.

The key to identifying desirable collateral is to analyse those simulations that cause the greatest increases in the potential exposure of the outstanding deals between the prior remarking and the end of the cure period. As mentioned in the section on Monte Carlo simulation, we can identify the deals whose changes in value contribute most to these largest changes in exposure. Alternatively, given the value of each risk factor in this subset of simulations, we can average these values over this subset and report the result in terms of the number of standard deviations from the mean. In the example given earlier in this chapter, analysis of the simulations one year in the future would highlight the fact that the largest increases in exposure were associated with several large US$/Euro forward FX transactions, caused by a 1.85 standard deviation average increase in the value of the Euro against the dollar. Given this information, it would be advantageous – in terms of minimizing net potential exposure – to encourage this counterparty to use government bonds denominated in Euros when posting collateral.

REHYPOTHECATION RISK

In the previous section, we were concerned with increases in net potential exposure between the prior remarking date and the end of the cure period. But we should also be concerned about significant decreases in this net exposure if we were required to post collateral at the prior remarking date. In this case, we have posted excess collateral and need to have it returned when the counterparty defaults. But if the counterparty has the right to rehypothecate the collateral (delivering the instruments received from us as collateral to a third party), or the collateral agreement includes transfer of the title of the pledged instruments, we may not be able to repossess the excess collateral and instead may have to file a claim for the excess collateral with the receiver. In this case, the posting of collateral may increase our exposure to the counterparty. But, by identifying the risk factor movements underlying the simulations which create the greatest decreases in the potential exposure of the outstanding deals between the prior remarking and the end of the cure period, we can choose to post collateral whose value decreases in these simulated states and thus minimise this problem.

THE USEFULNESS OF SIMULATING POTENTIAL CREDIT EXPOSURE WHEN REMARKING COLLATERAL DAILY

If collateral is remarked daily, the question can be raised: 'Rather than analyse potential credit exposure at each point in future time, why don't we just assume that the expected exposure is zero and the worst-case exposure equals the threshold amount, since daily remarking limits our losses to a minimal level?' If the cure period is only a day, if the values of the outstanding deals are unaffected by market and credit movements or if the outstanding deals and collateral are perfectly positively correlated, then it may be reasonable to ignore potential changes in value within the cure period. But there are many financial instruments, such as equity and interest rate options and credit swaps, whose values are highly sensitive to market movements, and ignoring the potential changes in their values over a cure period of a fortnight could seriously underestimate potential credit exposure. (In fact, one of the stronger arguments made for remarking collateral on a daily basis rests explicitly on the high price volatility of certain financial instruments.)

The other reason for modelling potential exposures at future points in time is to assist the management of collateral and liquidity. It was noted earlier in this chapter that negative deal values for non-nettable deals were often set to zero when calculating counterparty exposure. When simulating a collateral system, these negative values must be maintained, rather than eliminated, since they give rise to a demand for collateral by the counterparty. As shown earlier in this section, the collateral required to be posted to or demanded from the counterparty can be simulated at each future point in time. Aggregating these simulated amounts across counterparties can provide a forecast of collateral flows – how much collateral will be available for rehypothecation or will be demanded at future points in time. This forecasting exercise is useful for identifying significant collateral demands generated by negative exposures, and is of particular value in identifying the increases in collateral that would be required if the company were to suffer a rating downgrade which impacted collateral posting requirements.

CONCLUSION

Credit exposure is currently the largest source of risk for most banks. Netting can reduce this risk significantly for the major banks with significant derivatives portfolios, but collateral is the most important method available for significantly reducing credit risk over a wide range of financial instruments for most banks. Monte Carlo methods developed for simulating potential credit exposure at future points in time can be adapted to recognise the impact of both netting and collateral agreements on credit exposure. These methods can not only model the impact of a collateral programme on a counterparty's potential credit exposure profile, but can also model the effects of changing the many variables involved in setting up and managing a collateral programme. For example, these simulations can model changes in remarking periods, thresholds, haircuts, collateral enforceability, and so on, and can identify which types of eligible collateral are best at hedging against changes in the values of the deals outstanding with a given counterparty in the time between the last collateral remarking and the end of the cure period.

Banks striving to implement the 'Advanced' version of the 'Internal Rating Based Approach' to calculating the charges for credit risk proposed in the New Basel Capital Accord will find it essential to implement such simulation models if they hope to gain significant capital relief.

CHAPTER 11

THE IMPACT OF CAPITAL ADEQUACY REQUIREMENTS ON COLLATERAL MANAGEMENT

INTRODUCTION

One insight into the increasingly important role played by collateral in the credit risk management process is provided by a comparison between the amount of text devoted to collateral management in the 1988 Basel Accord on Credit Risk and in the new BIS Capital Adequacy Requirement proposal. Although the 1988 Basel Accord concentrates on the capital required to offset credit risks, to the exclusion of market and other risks, it only mentions collateral in one paragraph and one annex. By contrast, collateral is the subject of 48 of the 129 paragraphs devoted to the 'Standardised Approach' to credit risk in The New Basel Capital Accord, and a further 36 paragraphs of the 'Internal Ratings Based Approach' to credit risk are devoted to collateral issues.

The purpose of this chapter is, first, to summarise the constraints imposed on collateral managers by the Bank for International Settlement's approach to collateral management laid out in the 1988 Accord; second, to describe in detail the far greater role of collateral in mitigating credit risk proposed in Part 2, 'The First Pillar – Minimum Capital Requirements', of the new consultative document; and finally to discuss some of the new business opportunities that this proposal will make available to collateral managers. For example, the proposed collateral requirements will encourage collateral managers to make collateral choice decisions based on an explicit analysis of the trade-offs between the risks and rewards of alternative forms of eligible collateral.

THE 1988 BASEL ACCORD

In this Accord, loans are generally[12] given a risk weight of 100%, and therefore incur a minimum capital requirement of 8% of the notional amount outstanding of the loan. Paragraph 39 of the Accord reduces this risk weighting in certain circumstances, stating that loans secured against cash, OECD central bank securities and specified multilateral development bank securities 'will attract the weight given to the collateral' and that partially collateralised loans 'will attract low weights on the part that is fully collateralised'. The risk weighting for this collateral is set out in Annex 2, section (d), which states that 'claims collateralised by cash or OECD central government securities or guaranteed by OECD central governments' will carry a risk weight of 0%.

No other securities count as eligible collateral for the purposes of calculating minimum capital requirements. Different haircuts for different types of eligible collateral are not specified (and therefore the implied haircut for all eligible securities is zero), currency mismatches between credit exposures and collateral securities are ignored, and there is no recognition of either the period between collateral remarkings or the 'cure' period between a credit event and liquidation.

The 1988 Accord therefore provides no incentives to reduce credit risk by shortening the collateral remarking period. Furthermore, by treating all eligible OECD central government securities as equally creditworthy and ignoring currency mismatches, the Accord provides no incentives for collateral managers to differentiate between the interest rate, FX and credit risks of eligible securities offered as collateral, and does provide a definite incentive for collateral managers to seek out high coupon eligible securities to post as collateral, even though such securities are (almost by definition) likely to be more risky.

THE NEW BASEL CAPITAL ACCORD

The consultative document issued by the Basel Committee on Banking Supervision on 31 May 2002 offers financial institutions two broad approaches to calculate the minimum capital requirements for credit risk – the 'Standardised Approach' and the 'Internal Ratings Based (IRB) Approach'. This latter approach is further subdivided into the 'Foundation Approach' and the 'Advanced Approach', which differ in the degree to which supervisory rules for estimating risk components can be replaced by internal estimates of certain risk factors.

The standardised approach basically continues the 'loan equivalent' approach to measuring credit exposure set out in previous BIS publications, but greatly refines the risk-weighting scheme set out in the 1988 Accord. Credit ratings provided by 'external credit assessment institutions' are used to create a relatively wide range of risk weights, and the standardised approach allows a wider range of techniques for mitigating credit risk, such as taking collateral, buying credit derivatives and obtaining guarantees, to be recognised for regulatory capital purposes.

The foundation IRB approach differs from the standardised approach by allowing banks to use internal estimates of Probabilities of Default (PD) and by expanding the range of eligible collateral, and the advanced IRB approach differs from the foundation IRB approach by permitting banks to 'use internal estimates of three additional risk components: Loss Given Default (LGD), Exposure at Default (EAD) and the treatment of guarantees/credit derivatives'.

In general, all of these approaches provide far more scope for collateral management to affect the minimum capital requirements, and, by providing considerably more detailed treatments of collateral than the 1988 Accord, create economic incentives for collateral managers to manage the trade-off between risk and return more efficiently. However, in return for increasing the role of collateral in calculating the minimum capital requirements, the BIS also sets out a number of conditions that must be met before capital relief will be granted to any form of collateral. We therefore next turn to a discussion of these conditions.

THE MINIMUM CONDITIONS FOR CAPITAL RELIEF

Banks must meet certain legal, economic and risk management conditions before regulators will grant capital relief to collateral.

The BIS is particularly concerned that the legal mechanism controlling the collateral process is robust and that the lender has clear rights to liquidate or retain the collateral. Specifically, banks must have legal opinions confirming enforceability and must fulfil enforceability requirements (for example, by registering a security interest), ensure adequate collateral segregation by custodians and clearly document the procedures for timely collateral liquidation.

Although the New Accord does widen the range of eligible collateral to include bank and corporate securities, it also requires that there be no significant positive correlation between the collateral's value and the credit quality of the obligor, and specifically rules ineligible any securities issued by an entity related to the collateral provider.

Finally, the consultative document states that 'while collateral reduces credit risk, it simultaneously increases other risks to which banks are exposed, such as legal, operational, liquidity and market risks'. It therefore states that it is imperative that a bank's risk management process be robust, with especial emphasis on the 'management of concentration risk arising from the bank's use of collateral'. If a bank does satisfy its regulators that it meets these conditions, the regulatory treatment of collateral depends on the approach to calculating minimum capital requirements chosen by the bank.

THE TREATMENT OF COLLATERAL IN THE STANDARDISED APPROACH

Banks choosing the standardised approach will be further required to choose between two approaches to the treatment of collateral – the 'simple approach' and the 'comprehensive approach'.

The list of eligible collateral for both the simple and comprehensive approach is, with some exceptions for securities issued by lower-rated government agencies, far longer than the list set out in paragraph 39 of the 1988 Accord. To cash and securities rated BB– and above issued by sovereigns and public sector entities are added bank, securities firm and corporate securities rated BBB– and above, equities listed on recognised exchanges and gold. But, given that less creditworthy securities are now eligible, both the simple and comprehensive approaches have taken pains to recognise the differential impact on minimum capital calculations of the various risk classes of eligible collateral and of alternative styles of collateral management.

THE SIMPLE STANDARDISED APPROACH

In the simple approach, eligible collateral that is pledged for the life of the offsetting exposure and re-valued to market at least semi-annually will be recognised. The collateralised portion of a claim will, as in the current Accord, attract the risk weight applicable to the collateral instrument, but with one important condition. Rather than allowing the 0% weight detailed in Annex 2 of the 1988 Accord, the weight will be subject to a 20% floor unless certain conditions are met.

These conditions are set out in detail in paragraphs 108–10. In order to get a 10% weight, a bank must meet certain conditions related to legal enforceability, the exposure and collateral must be denominated in the same currency and marked-to-market and re-margined daily, the cure period must not exceed 10 days, the bank's claim must not have a risk weight exceeding 20% in the standardised approach and one side of the transaction must have a 0% weight. To qualify for a 0% weight, tighter conditions must be met – the transaction must be a repo-style transaction, both the claim and the collateral must qualify for a 0% weight, and the cure period must not exceed 4 days.

In summary, the simple standardised approach makes a much wider range of securities eligible for collateral purposes, but imposes tougher conditions that must be met if a low risk weight is to be attained. In particular, the simple approach provides a strong incentive for banks desiring a low risk weight to mark-to-market and re-margin transactions daily. If a transaction is not marked-to-market and re-margined daily, it can still attract a 0% weight, but only if the collateral posted is either cash in the same currency or a security, issued by a 0% weight sovereign, whose market value has been discounted by 30%.

THE COMPREHENSIVE STANDARDISED APPROACH

Collateral also reduces risk weights in the comprehensive approach, but this risk weighting scheme is not based on the risk weight of the posted collateral, but rather adjusts the risk weight of the uncollateralised exposure, r.

It starts with the market value of the collateral posted, C. This market value is then reduced by several 'haircuts', which recognise the volatilities of the collateral and the uncollateralised exposure and any currency volatility, to produce the 'adjusted value of the collateral', C_A. These haircuts can be calculated in two ways: a 'standard' approach and an 'own estimates'[13] approach. Table 11.1 lays out the haircuts used in the standard approach.

The adjusted value of collateral is then calculated using the equation set out in paragraph 85:

$$C_A = \frac{C}{1 + H_E + H_C + H_{FX}}$$

where H_E, H_C and H_{FX} are the haircuts appropriate to the exposure, collateral and foreign exchange volatilities respectively. The capital relief granted by this scheme to collateral is therefore very dependent on the severity of the haircuts applied to the market value of the collateral.

This adjusted value, C_A, is then compared with the market value of the uncollateralised exposure, E. If this exposure is fully collateralised by the adjusted value of the collateral ($C_A \geq E$), the adjusted risk weight is set as a percentage, w,[14] of r and the final 'risk-weighted asset'[15] for this exposure equals r * w * E. If the adjusted value of the collateral only partially collateralises the exposure ($C_A < E$), then the risk weight is set equal to $r*\{1 - (1-w) * C_A/E\}$.

Table 11.1 Haircuts for the Standardised Approach (assuming daily mark-to-market and re-margining)

Debt securities	Residual maturity	Sovereigns %	Banks and corporates %
AAA/AA	≤ 1 year	0.5	1
	> 1 year, ≤ 5 years	2	4
	> 5 years	4	8
A/BBB	≤ 1 year	1	2
	> 1 year, ≤ 5 years	3	6
	> 5 years	6	12
BB	≤ 1 year	20	–
	> 1 year, ≤ 5 years	20	–
	> 5 years	20	–
Main index equities			20
Other equities listed on a recognised exchange			30
Gold			15
Cash			0
Surcharge for foreign exchange risk			8

Under this scheme, for every increase in the adjusted value of collateral equal to 1% of the exposure, the exposure is reduced by 0.85%, to the point where, if the adjusted value of the collateral equals 100% or more of the exposure, the exposure is reduced by 85%.

The standard haircut approach also differentiates between 'capital market-driven transactions' (whose documentation contains re-margining clauses) and secured lending transactions (whose documentation generally does not) when the frequency of re-margining is less than daily. For capital market-driven transactions with longer re-margining frequencies, the 'benchmark' haircuts given in Table 11.1 are modified in the following manner:

$$H = H_{10} * \{(N_{RM} + 9)/10\}^{1/2}$$

where H_{10} is the (10 business day) benchmark haircut and N_{RM} is the actual number of days between revaluations. For similar secured lending transactions, the haircut is:

$$H = H_{10} * \{(N_{RM} + 19)/10\}^{1/2}$$

with a maximum of six months between collateral re-markings. Thus, in the worst case of a loan secured by equities listed on a recognised exchange, quoted in a different currency and re-valued semi-annually, H_C would rise from 30% to approximately 135% and H_{FX} climb from 8% to approximately 34%.

The comprehensive approach also provides for a reduction in the value of the floor factor, w, from 15% to 0% under conditions, set out in paragraph 102, which are almost identical to those required to qualify for a 0% weight in the simple approach. A further reduction is permitted for transactions that qualify for this 'zero w' treatment. If the counterparty is a 'core market participant',[16] as defined in paragraph 104, supervisors may apply a zero H to these transactions. In these circumstances, the adjusted value of the collateral, C_A, is set equal to the market value of the collateral, C, and, if the exposure is fully collateralised, the final risk-weighted asset for minimum capital charge purposes is reduced to zero.

In summary, the comprehensive approach also provides incentives to mark-to-market and re-margin transactions daily, and recognises the same eligible collateral instruments as the simple approach. However, by replacing the simple approach's use of the risk weight of the collateral with the haircut approach, the comprehensive approach allows for a much finer differentiation between risk weights and encourages collateral managers to consider the economic trade-offs between the various forms of collateral in more detail.

DERIVING RISK-WEIGHTED ASSETS UNDER THE INTERNAL RATINGS BASED APPROACH

The risk weight categories for the standardised approach set out in paragraphs 23–44 are considerably more refined than the broad categories used in the 1988 Accord, but the methodology used to calculate risk weights in the foundation and advanced IRB approaches is even more detailed.[17] In the foundation IRB approach, the risk weight of a transaction depends on the bank's internal estimate of the Probability of Default (PD) associated with the borrower's grade and the supervisor's estimate of the Loss Given Default (LGD) for that corporate exposure. In the advanced approach,[18] qualifying banks may also use internal estimates of LGD and Exposure at Default (EAD). That the BIS believes that the advanced approach will lead to lower minimum capital levels than the foundation approach is made clear by the requirement that, for two years following the date of implementation of the New Accord, the capital requirement calculated using the advanced approach is subject to floor of 90% of the capital requirement calculated using the foundation approach.

In both of these approaches, the credit enhancement provided by guarantees and credit derivatives are recognised by making adjustments to the obligor's probability of default. In contrast, eligible collateral mitigates credit risk by reducing the LGD of a transaction.

THE TREATMENT OF COLLATERAL IN THE FOUNDATION IRB APPROACH

The range of eligible collateral in this approach expands on the standardised approach's list (hereafter referred to as eligible financial collateral) by including commercial and real estate collateral (hereafter referred to as eligible physical collateral) that meets minimum requirements, set out in paragraphs 310–21, covering legal certainty, the correlation between collateral and exposure and the risk management process.

The methodology for measuring the impact of eligible financial collateral is very similar to the methodology used in the comprehensive standardised approach. Haircuts are calculated in the same manner, as is the adjusted value of the collateral. The impact of collateral on LGD in the foundation IRB approach is completely analogous to its impact on risk weights in the comprehensive standardised approach, and the conditions for applying a 'zero w' and 'zero H' to transactions are identical.

The treatment of eligible physical collateral follows the same methodology, but is harsher. Whereas the effective LGD is reduced to 15% of the original LGD when the exposure is fully collateralised by financial collateral, it is only reduced to 40% when the exposure is fully collateralised by physical collateral.[18] When banks take both financial and physical collateral against a corporate exposure, the exposure is split into a part secured by the financial collateral and another part secured by the physical collateral. The appropriate LGDs are then calculated for each part and summed to give the effective LGD for the corporate exposure.

In summary, the foundation IRB approach expands the range of collateral deemed eligible under the standardised approach to include physical collateral, calculates the impact of eligible collateral using the same haircut-based methodology as the standardised approach and, by using risk weights based on Loss Given Default numbers and allowing banks to estimate Probabilities of Default, moves even further towards a more refined system of collateral management.

THE TREATMENT OF COLLATERAL IN THE ADVANCED IRB APPROACH

Given that the banks that qualify for the advanced IRB approach will be allowed to use internal estimates of Loss Given Default, Exposure at Default and the treatment of guarantees and credit derivatives, it is understandable that the minimum requirements for institutions choosing this approach are more rigorous than those required for institutions using the foundation IRB approach.

The advanced IRB approach to collateral management requires conservative minimum operational standards, stating in paragraph 364 that the bank 'must establish internal requirements for legal certainty and the risk management process that are, at the least, consistent with those required for the standardised and foundation approaches', but does permit institutions considerable leeway in modelling collateral, stating in paragraph 344 that 'A bank is responsible for determining the appropriate techniques for how collateral is factored into its LGD estimates'. The paragraph continues by noting that the bank must consider, and address in a conservative manner, issues such as collateral price volatility, collateral price quote frequency, the correlation between the exposure and the collateral, collateral concentration, currency mismatches, the workout period and a bank's 'ability to liquidate collateral expeditiously where the collateral remains in the possession and under the control of the borrower'.

In summary, the advanced IRB approach allows a bank to develop a credit risk management system that is economically based, and which therefore provides excellent incentives for collateral to be managed using marginal economic analysis. One fly in the ointment in this approach will be the requirement that banks will still be required to use the 'Potential Exposure' add-ons set out in Annex 3 of the 1988 Accord as estimates of Exposure at Default for derivatives. These exposure numbers can be very different from the credit exposures estimated using Monte Carlo analysis, and thus will be a bone of contention, 'for the time being', for banks with considerable derivatives exposures.

CONCLUSION

The 1988 Accord covers collateral quite lightly, using a very simple model. Only cash and securities issued by OECD central banks and specified multilateral development banks count as eligible collateral, and the 1988 Accord ignores many issues that affect the degree of coverage provided by the collateral.[19] Under this regime, it is quite easy to understand why a collateral management group charged with managing securities and derivatives exposure could choose to deal only in one government's securities.

The New Basel Capital Accord pays far more attention to the collateral management process. The standardised approach expands the list of eligible collateral, but explicitly recognises that poorly managed collateral programmes can increase the risks to which banks are exposed, and therefore devotes considerable space to the minimum standards that banks will have to meet in order to qualify for capital relief. For example, the consultative document spends eight paragraphs detailing the minimum conditions for capital relief under the standardised approach. The foundation IRB approach further expands the list of eligible collateral to include physical assets, but then imposes additional minimum operational requirements focusing on maximising recoveries from collateral liquidation, reorganisation and bankruptcy. Clarity about the legal process underpinning collateral agreements will be essential (creating an increased emphasis on the careful negotiation of collateral documents), and the bank's collateral management processes will be carefully scrutinised.

The expansion of the list of eligible collateral will obviously help to resolve any liquidity problems engendered by demands for government securities,[20] and the inclusion of physical assets as eligible collateral in the foundation IRB approach will provide an additional incentive for banks to accept commercial real estate as collateral; but the most immediate impact of this expansion, in combination with haircuts linked to collateral price volatility, remarking periods and currency risk, will be the introduction of incentives to manage collateral on an economic basis.

Under the 1988 Accord, corporate bonds are not accepted as collateral for the purposes of calculating minimum capital requirements. By allowing these securities to be posted, with higher haircuts, as collateral in lieu of sovereign debt, the New Accord may create a 'win–win' situation. The receiver of the collateral may believe that the larger amount posted may more than offset any increased price volatility over the relevant remarking period, and the provider of the collateral may be happy to post the larger amount of a security that is paying a higher return.

Under the 1988 Accord, Euro exposures collateralised with US$ government bonds receive a 0% risk weight, ignoring the collateral value shortfall that would be caused by a decrease in the value of the US$. The New Accord explicitly provides an incentive to minimise this foreign exchange risk – a BBB-rated, 7-year corporate bond has a 12% haircut when it is hedging an exposure in the same currency, but a BBB-rated, 7-year sovereign bond has a total haircut of 14% (6% + 8%) when it is hedging an exposure in a foreign currency.

For smaller banks concerned about the costs involved in remarking collateral daily, the New Accord allows for an explicit trade-off to be made between the amount of collateral posted and the remarking period. Increasing the remarking period to one month approximately doubles the haircut, and a three-month remarking period trebles the haircut. But these haircuts mean that, rather than dividing the value of a one-year, AA-rated corporate bond by 1.01 when calculating the adjusted collateral value, the divisors are 1.02 and 1.03 respectively.

By significantly reducing the divergences between the collateral management policies that reduce economic risk capital and those that reduce regulatory risk capital, the New Basel Capital Accord creates strong incentives for financial institutions to manage collateral rationally; and, according to the 2002 ISDA Margin Survey, the participants have already begun to respond to these incentives.

COLLATERAL RISK MANAGEMENT

As we have noted throughout this book, taking collateral mitigates credit risk, but when we take collateral, we actually exchange that credit risk for a series of new risks which must be measured, monitored and managed as professionally as credit risk itself. Chapter 12 looks at some of the major risks involved in the collateralisation process and makes some suggestions for appropriate metrics and risk management techniques. This is presented in tabular form (Table 12.1).

Table 12.1 Major risks in the collateralisation process

Agreement structure risk

Definition	Metrics	Risk management techniques
Agreement structure risk is the risk that a collateral agreement is structured such as to give rise to risks in the collateral management process rather than to mitigate them. An example might be that the negotiator includes terms which cannot be easily monitored, for example unsecured thresholds based on a hedge fund's Net Asset Value.	Suitable metrics for this risk might include (i) recording exemptions agreed to the collateral policy or (ii) the collateral operations team tracking the agreements which require significant manual intervention.	Recommended risk management techniques include (i) having a well-documented collateral policy (ii) controlling carefully the number and type of people who can agree exceptions to the policy and (iii) having flexible collateral management technology which can support different types of parameters.

Operating risks

Along with legal risks, operating risks in the collateral management process are some of the most important risks to manage.

Definition	Metrics	Risk management techniques
Operating risks are any of the risks which occur during the collateral management process which mean that incorrect amounts of collateral are held vis-à-vis exposure in a default situation, and that such a deficit has not been recorded or accounted for in credit risk management systems. Two of the major operating risks are (i) that collateral calls are not made on time, or at all and (ii) that when collateral calls are made, they are not correct because either trades are missing from the exposure calculations or trade mark-to-market information is incorrect.	Suitable metrics for this risk might include (i) tracking and reporting the number of collateral calls which are not made on time or (ii) recording the number of disputes which arise with counterparties owing to the collateral requirements being calculated incorrectly.	Recommended risk management techniques include (i) staffing the collateral management team with expert professionals (ii) controlling carefully the number and type of people who can agree exceptions to the policy and (iii) having controls in place to ensure that all trades are captured by the collateral management system either automatically or manually.

cont'd

Table 12.1 continued

Settlement risk

Definition	Metrics	Risk management techniques
Settlement risk is the risk that collateral deliveries are not made on time, or at all.	A suitable metric for this risk is a report which documents actual settlements, and settlement timing versus what was scheduled or expected.	The recommended risk management technique for this risk is to have either a very close link between the collateral management team and the settlements area including detailed and frequent communication, or automated linkages between the settlements systems and the collateral management system.

Market risk

Definition	Metrics	Risk management techniques
Market risk in collateral management is the risk that the collateral balance is not sufficient to offset exposure either because the portfolio mark-to-market has increased in value, or the collateral holdings have declined in value.	A suitable metric for market risk is a daily report which shows collateral holdings vis-à-vis unsecured exposures taking into account documented parameters such as unsecured thresholds.	There are two primary risk management techniques for market risk. The first is to call for collateral every day and ensure that it settles quickly e.g. by limiting eligible collateral to cash. The second is to ensure that the haircuts on collateral assets are set taking into account historic volatility and expected future volatility to ensure that the actual amounts of collateral act as a cushion to changes in portfolio and collateral market value between collateral calls.

Table 12.1 continued

Liquidity risk

Definition	Metrics	Risk management techniques
Liquidity risk in this context is the risk that activities and structures in the collateral management programme cause liquidity pressure within the organisation. An example of this is the presence of credit rating-dependent thresholds in collateral agreements which mean that upon a downgrade a firm needs to pledge additional collateral at precisely the same time as their funding costs increase.	The appropriate metric for liquidity risk is a report which shows how much additional collateral the firm needs to deliver in the event of credit rating downgrades.	Prevention is the best form of cure for liquidity risk. When agreeing to rating-dependent thresholds, firms should ensure that the extent of the change in the threshold becomes gradually less with any larger steps taking place between, say, AAA and AA.

Concentration risk

Definition	Metrics	Risk management techniques
Concentration risk is the risk that the collateral that a firm holds against its portfolio of collateralised agreements is focused in a few asset types or currencies. An example would include holding more than 50% of a company's equity across all a firm's collateral agreements. This becomes a problem in the event that the issuer of the collateral defaults, or in the event of counterparty defaults when collateral assets need to be sold, possibly in a hurry.	Concentration risk can be measured using simple reports which show a sum of all collateral held in the portfolio by type, both across the portfolio and also in relation to individual collateral agreements.	Concentration risk can be managed by ensuring that a firm's policy on eligible collateral is to limit it to high-quality collateral (e.g. G7 government bonds) or cash. Additionally, if risk management reports show high degrees of concentration, collateral assets can be hedged in the same way as other financial instruments.

cont'd

Table 12.1 continued

Correlation risk

Definition	Metrics	Risk management techniques
Correlation risk is the risk that there is a high degree of connectivity between the collateral and the giver of that collateral. Examples of correlation risk include a corporate delivering its own shares as collateral, or a corporate delivering its own weakly rated government bonds.	Correlation risk can be measured using management reports which show deliveries of collateral by counterparty. Users may wish to sort the reports by countries, currencies and industrial sectors.	Correlation risk can also be managed by ensuring that a firm's policy controls eligible collateral to limit potential correlation risk. And again, correlation risk can be managed by hedging collateral assets.

Legal risks

Along with operating risk, legal risk is one of the critical risks which a collateral manager should focus on.

Definition	Metrics	Risk management techniques
Legal risk is the risk that in the event of the default of a collateralised counterparty that the arrangement is not upheld by the bankruptcy judge managing the proceedings. Collateral agreements may not be recognised in the jurisdiction in question, the collateral agreement may not conform with the local laws or it may have been operated in such a way as to have voided the agreement.	The metric for managing legal risk is the documentation of any divergences from legal best practices in collateral agreements or in the way that those agreements are operated.	Legal risk has to be managed by ensuring that a firm's collateral programme is run in accordance with legal opinions on collateral management. Such opinions may be industry standard or bespoke. Firms may also address legal risk by taking account of it, quantitatively, in their credit risk management systems.

NOTES

1   International Swaps and Derivatives Association (ISDA) Margin Survey 2002 and 2001.
2   ISDA Margin Survey 2002.
3   If a party is 'in-the-money' it means that the net present value of all the cashflows outstanding between the party and their counterparty is positive, which means that if all the outstanding trades were closed out (or if the counterparty defaulted) it would result in a net cash payment to the party.
4   The ISDA Credit Support Annex and other forms of collateral documentation are covered in Chapter 5.
5   Mark-to-market is the net present value of all outstanding cash flows of a transaction based on current market rates and parameters.
6   These terms, which can be found in the ISDA Credit Support Annex, will be examined in more detail in Chapter 5.
7   The Basel Committee on Banking Supervision is perhaps the most influential committee of the Bank for International Settlements (BIS – Basel, Switzerland). The BIS is the world's oldest international financial institution and remains the principal forum for international central bank co-operation.
8   A bank's FX settlement exposure runs from the time that its payment order for the currency sold can no longer be recalled or cancelled with certainty – the unilateral payment cancellation deadline – and lasts until the time that the currency purchased is received with finality. Because of the difficulty of cancelling payment orders, this period can in fact last for a number of days.
9   Novation is the substitution of a new debt for an old debt and includes the cancellation of the old debt. It is the most final and therefore legally the cleanest form of debt transfer.
10   Meridien Research as quoted in Wall Street Technology online (Feb 2002).
11   ISDA Margin Survey 2001.
12   The risk weight for loans that are 'fully secured by a mortgage on residential property that is or will be occupied by the borrower or that is rented' is reduced to 50%.
For sovereigns, the risk weights will be more conservative than those in the current system, ranging from 0% for sovereigns rated AA– and higher by Standard & Poor's to 150% for sovereigns rated below B–. The risk weights will also be more conservative for banks under either of the two options that national supervisors will apply to all banks in their jurisdiction. Under the first option, all banks will be assigned a risk weight that

depends on their country's rating (for example, if a sovereign's rating is in the range A+ to A–, with a risk weight of 20%, then the banks will be assigned the 50% risk weight appropriate for sovereigns whose ratings range from BBB+ to BBB–). The second option bases a bank's risk weight on its credit rating, ranging from 20% for banks rated AA– or higher to 150% for banks rated below B–. By contrast, although the new system increases the risk weight for corporations rated below BB– to 150%, it reduces the risk weight to 50% for corporations rated between A+ and A–, and to 20% for corporations rated AA– or higher.

13 Banks may be permitted to use their own haircut estimates if they use an internal market risk model under the 1996 Market Risk Amendment and meet the additional requirements pertaining to collateral illiquidity and non-normal distributions set out in paragraphs 92–5.

14 The January 2001 draft of the consultative document set this percentage, w, at 15%. The value of this 'floor' factor may be reduced in future drafts.

15 A risk-weighted asset, RWA, is defined as the risk weight of a transaction multiplied by a measure of exposure for that transaction.

16 Core market participants may include sovereigns, central banks and PSEs; banks and security firms; other financial companies (including insurance companies) eligible for a 20% risk weight; regulated mutual funds that are subject to capital or leverage requirements; regulated pension funds; and recognised clearing organisations.

17 The equations for calculating the risk weight in the foundation approach are set out in paragraphs 173 and 174, linking it to LGD and PD. For the advanced approach, and when there is an explicit maturity dimension in the foundation approach, the equation in paragraph 173 is replaced with the equation in paragraph 177, which includes an exposure maturity factor.

18 However, the consultative document states, in paragraph 367, that 'For the time being, no bank will be permitted to use its own estimates of credit equivalent amounts of interest rate, foreign exchange, equity and commodity derivatives – instead the current matrix of add-ons will continue to apply.'

19 One of the operational requirements is that the bank should have a distinct operational unit devoted to collateral management. Another is that the bank should perform stress tests that cover economic or industry downturns, market shocks and liquidity crises, and that especial attention should be paid to the impact of mass rating downgrades, higher default rates and lower recovery rates.

20 Such as collateral price volatility, the time between re-margining, the correlation between the exposure and the collateral, collateral and exposure currency mismatches and the cure period.

INDEX

Printed in the United States
154018LV00002B/6/A